insight text guide

Niki Cook

Looking for Alibrandi

Melina Marchetta

insight®

▸innovative ▸engaging ▸evolving

First published in 2023, reprinted in 2023.

Insight Publications Pty Ltd
3/350 Charman Road
Cheltenham VIC 3192
Australia
Tel: +61 3 8571 4950
Fax: +61 3 8571 0257
Email: books@insightpublications.com.au

www.insightpublications.com.au

A catalogue record for this book is available from the National Library of Australia

Melina Marchetta's Looking for Alibrandi / Niki Cook

Niki Cook asserts the moral right to be identified as the author of this work.

ISBNs:
9781922771025 (print)
9781922771032 (digital)
9781922771049 (bundle: print + digital)

Cover design by Melisa Paredes

Printed by Markono Print Media Pte Ltd

contents

CHARACTER MAP

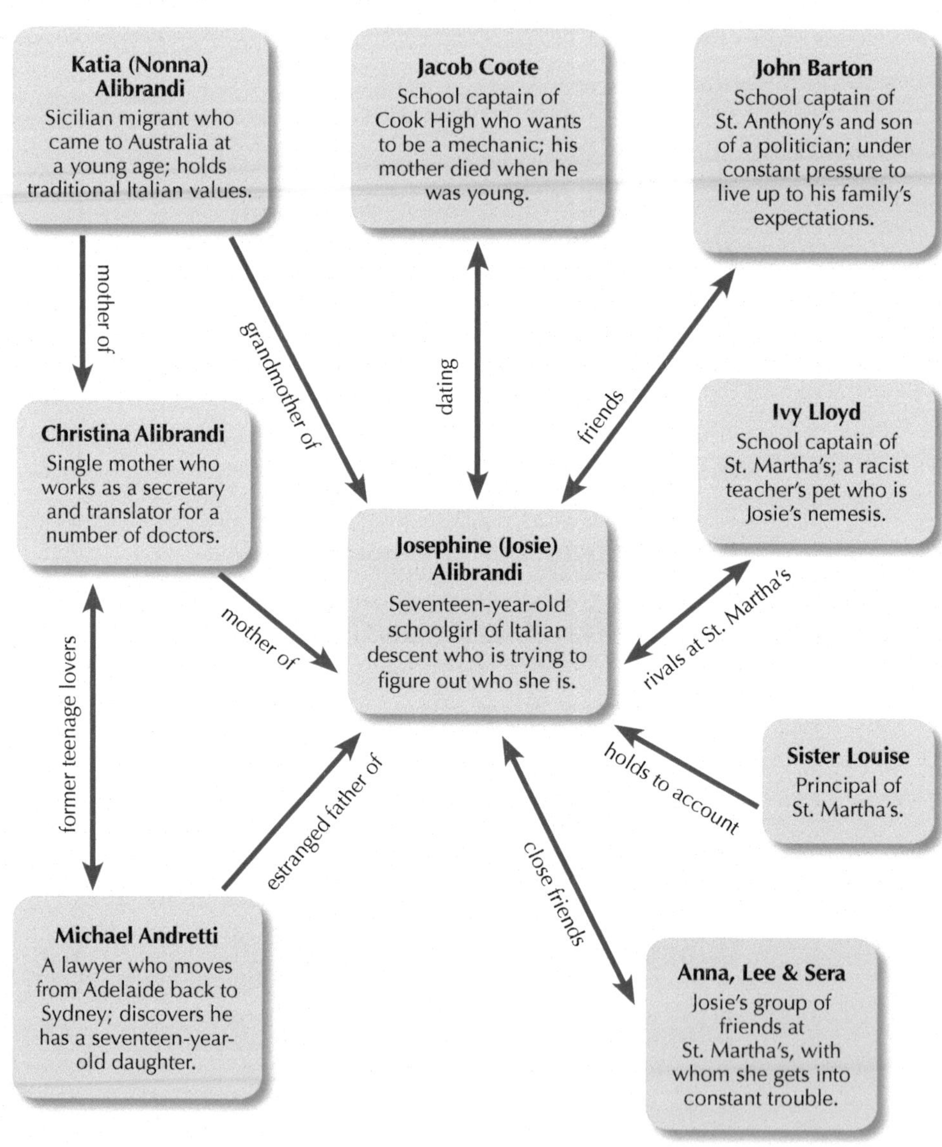

OVERVIEW

About the author

Born in Sydney in 1965, Melina Marchetta is of Italian descent. She attended Rosebank College but left at the age of fifteen. She subsequently attended business school, before working for the Commonwealth Bank and then a travel agency. She returned to study and completed a teaching degree at the Australian Catholic University. She subsequently taught English, History and Italian at St. Mary's Cathedral College for ten years, before focusing on writing full-time.

Looking for Alibrandi is Marchetta's first novel, written while she was still working at the bank. It was rejected by publishers six times in seven years, before finally being published in 1992. *Looking for Alibrandi* was released to widespread acclaim, winning a number of awards including the CBCA Children's Book of the Year Award for older readers. Marchetta also wrote the screenplay for the 1999 film adaptation of the novel, for which she won an Australian Film Institute award for Best Adapted Script.

After a significant gap after the success of her first novel, many of Marchetta's books for children and young adults have been published. These include *Saving Francesca* (2003), *On the Jellicoe Road* (2006), *Finnikin of the Rock* (2008) and the *What Zola Did* series (2020–21). She has won, or been shortlisted for, a range of awards for her fiction writing.

Synopsis

The novel begins on Josie's first day of her final year of high school at St. Martha's, a prestigious Catholic girls' school. When Josie returns home that evening, her mother, Christina, reveals that Michael Andretti, Josie's father, has returned to Sydney. He is unaware of Josie's existence, having moved to Adelaide with his family as a teenager, shortly after Josie's conception.

School events dominate Josie's life. She and her friends, Sera, Lee and Anna, three girls at St. Martha's who she considers fellow misfits, attend 'Have a Say Day' in central Sydney. Josie gives a speech, and meets the attractive Jacob Coote, school captain of Cook High. At the start of the debating season, Josie meets up with John Barton, a friend she has a crush on. John is school captain of St. Anthony's, and comes from a privileged background. His father is a politician, and John is expected to follow in his footsteps; however, he doesn't want to do this, and reveals to Josie that he hates his life. Later, at the regional school dance, Josie dances with Jacob, who takes her home on his motorbike at the end of the night. She is intrigued by Jacob, but disappointed that she doesn't get to dance with John.

Having briefly encountered Michael Andretti one afternoon at her grandmother's house, Josie meets her father properly at a family barbecue. She confronts him angrily, and they agree to stay out of each other's lives. At the same event, Josie's grandmother, Nonna Katia, realises that Michael is Josie's father.

Shortly afterwards, at school, Josie breaks Carly Bishop's nose with a book after Carly insults her. Josie calls Michael, who is a barrister, to get her out of trouble, which, to Josie's surprise, he does.

While spending her afternoons with Nonna Katia, with whom she has a fractious relationship, Josie learns about Katia's immigration journey, her early years in Australia and the hardships she faced. Katia reveals she met an Australian policeman, Marcus Sandford, who treated her kindly. As Josie's tolerance of her grandmother improves, her relationship with her mother deteriorates, as Josie reacts negatively to Christina dating.

Josie agrees to go out with Jacob after he saves her from a bully while she is working at McDonald's, but only if he meets her mother. He reluctantly agrees, but when he shows up both his manner and appearance are offensive. Josie walks out on the date, and fortuitously runs into Michael, who takes her for pizza and then safely home, after offering her an after-school job at his law firm.

Josie bumps into John again, who is even more depressed than before. They write down their feelings in sealed envelopes and exchange them, to be opened after their end-of-year HSC exams. Josie and Jacob make up and agree to go on another date, skipping school to do so. After this date, Josie decides she's in love.

Josie spends more time with Michael, visiting his family in Adelaide during the holidays. She learns more about him, and about his relationship with Christina when they were young.

At 'Tomato Day', Josie's family gets together to make pasta sauce. Nonna Katia and her sister Patrizia recount how Marcus Sandford helped them during WWII when the men were interned. They discuss how Patrizia, her husband and Francesco moved to Sydney for work, leaving Katia alone in Queensland over Christmas.

Josie and her friends skip the annual St. Martha's walk-a-thon in an attempt to see a celebrity, meaning Josie abandons her leadership responsibilities. Sister Louise reprimands Josie for her behaviour and reveals she was actually voted school captain, but that Sister Louise had doubts about her, so gave the position to Ivy Lloyd instead. Josie is upset, but realises she is more popular than she thinks.

Josie and Jacob's relationship develops, but he is angry when she goes to the cinema with John. She visits his house and they become intimate in his room but argue when she refuses to have sex with him.

At Christina's birthday party, the family joke about her being conceived over the Christmas–New Year period. This leads to Josie realising that Francesco cannot be Christina's father. She angrily confronts Katia, who admits that Marcus Sandford is Christina's real father. Josie is angry for a week, but then asks Katia to explain, and she reveals Francesco was an unpleasant husband and also impotent. He agreed to raise Christina as his own to save face, but this negatively impacted Christina's relationship with both Katia and Francesco.

Shortly before the final exams, Josie sees John at a rugby match, and he is upbeat and playful, in contrast to his recent depressive state. However, the next day, a distraught Ivy reveals to Josie that John has killed himself. Josie struggles with the news, oscillating from disbelief to anger. She opens the letter he gave her, and then rips it up. Jacob also finds John's death hard to take. His death does, however, enable Josie and Ivy to realise that they are more similar than either would admit.

Jacob breaks up with Josie, believing that they both need to figure out who they are. Josie is distraught but realises that this is the final piece in her emancipation. Having struggled with her identity throughout, she is able to find peace in who she is and her relationships.

Character summaries

Josephine (Josie) Alibrandi

The narrator and protagonist of the novel, Josie is aged seventeen and in her final year at St. Martha's. She is the illegitimate daughter of Christina and Michael, and has been raised by her mother, with no contact with her father until the events of the novel.

Christina Alibrandi

Mother of Josie and daughter of Katia, Christina is thirty-four years old, having had Josie when she was seventeen.

Katia (Nonna) Alibrandi

Sicilian-born Katia came to Australia as a seventeen-year-old, accompanying her husband Francesco.

Michael Andretti

Josie's father Michael dated Christina when they were teenagers. He was unaware that he had a daughter.

John Barton

Seventeen-year-old John is the son of Robert Barton, a politician, and part of a family with a long history in Australian politics.

Jacob Coote

Jacob is the school captain of Cook High, a public school, and he lives in Redfern with his father. He dates Josie.

Ivy Lloyd

School captain of St. Martha's, Ivy is Josie's nemesis.

Seraphina (Sera)

One of Josie's close friends at St. Martha's, Sera is also of Italian heritage.

Lee Taylor

Lee is another of Josie's close friends and the quietest of the four.

Anna Selicic

Anna is the 'baby' of the friendship group and the most naive.

Sister Louise

The principal of St. Martha's, she has high expectations of Josie and holds her to account for her behaviour.

Greg Sims

Greg is a bully who used to live next door to Josie when she was ten.

Roberto (Robert)

Josie's cousin Roberto attends St. Anthony's alongside John Barton.

Anton Valavic

One of Jacob's friends from Cook High, Anton goes out with Anna.

Francesco Alibrandi

The deceased husband of Katia, Francesco does not directly appear in the novel, but looms large nonetheless.

Zia (Aunt) Patrizia and Zio (Uncle) Ricardo

Katia's sister and brother-in-law, these members of the extended Italian family live in Sydney.

Marcus Sandford

Marcus is the Australian policeman/army officer who befriended Katia in Queensland. He is also Christina's biological father.

Carly Bishop

A student in Josie's year at St. Martha's, Carly is also a part-time model.

Paul Presilio

Paul is Christina's boss, with whom she goes on a date.

BACKGROUND & CONTEXT

Looking for Alibrandi takes place in inner Sydney in the early 1990s and contains a number of contemporary references to the popular culture and geography of the time. While elements of Australian culture have remained consistent, some things have changed considerably in the last thirty or so years, and therefore some references may be unfamiliar to modern readers. Knowledge of the history of immigration, multiculturalism and the social divides within Sydney (and Australia more generally) will be useful when developing an understanding of the key themes of the novel.

Italian migration to Australia

Migration from Italy to Australia was limited during the nineteenth century, with small numbers arriving during the 1840s and 1850s. It was a long, slow journey, taking over two months, and there was no direct shipping link between Australia and Italy until the end of the century. The majority of Italians who migrated in these early years were from rural backgrounds, and many settled in Queensland as canecutters, or found work in mining in Western Australia. Numbers gradually increased with the turn of the century, and the 1911 census recorded 6719 residents who listed Italy as their country of birth.

Following World War I, stricter controls were placed on Italian migration to the US, which led many Italian immigrants to choose to relocate to Australia instead. Roughly 30 000 Italians arrived in Australia between 1922 and 1930, and by the 1933 census Italians were the largest non-English speaking ethnic group in Australia. The migrants who arrived were overwhelmingly male, and they sought to establish themselves financially before being joined by their wives, children and wider family in subsequent years.

From the early days of migration, there was tension between Australians and the Italian settlers. Italian migrants were the targets of racism, and often encountered prejudice and resentment. This increased in the early 1930s, as the Great Depression created economic challenges across the world, including in Australia. There were riots in Kalgoorlie in Western Australia in 1934, resulting from a clash between Italian migrants and Anglo Australians, which led to the burning of a number of homes and businesses owned by Italians and other southern Europeans.

The outbreak of World War II intensified the existing divisions between Italian migrants and other white Australians. There had already been negativity brewing due to Benito Mussolini's fascist policies during the 1930s, but Italy's entry into the war as an ally of Germany led to the internment of many resident Italians in camps within Australia, predominantly in Queensland, Western Australia and South Australia. Additionally, over 18 000 Italian prisoners of war were sent to internment camps in Australia, and these prisoners were largely employed on inland farms.

Following the end of World War II, migration from Italy increased significantly. Post-war Italy was in a poor state economically and physically, and its infrastructure had been devastated. The return of soldiers from war also resulted in a high rate of unemployment, and thus many chose to seek opportunities elsewhere. From the early 1950s, Australia operated a system of personal recommendations, where current residents could nominate others, thus allowing families to be reunited; this system also had the intention of ensuring that those who entered Australia were of good repute. In the second half of the twentieth century, almost 391 000 migrants arrived from Italy.

Since 1980, Italian migration has slowed considerably; however, a resurgence in economic hardship in Italy in recent years has seen a new wave of migration within the last decade.

Attitudes to Italian migrants

Italian migrants were subject to considerable prejudice and racism from the early days of Italian immigration to Australia. While they were viewed as being preferable to non-white migrants, they were still viewed as inferior due to a perceived 'primitive' way of life.

The most popular method of migration was 'chain migration', which involved people from the same village or town migrating and settling in the same area. The men typically came first, and then were followed by wives and other relatives. This maintenance of established societies provided security and solace for the migrants, but often caused conflict within Australian communities because of segregation and the perceived unwillingness of migrants to assimilate.

Italian culture

Having a basic knowledge of some elements of Italian culture will help you to understand the conflicting expectations that Josie feels are placed upon her.

Reputation plays a significant role in Italian culture. The impression that a person leaves on others is of great importance, and it is seen to reflect on their family and their upbringing. Knowing how to behave in different situations, being polite, gaining social approval, and conducting oneself appropriately are all seen as important virtues.

Family plays a central role in Italian culture. There is a focus on extended family, and family gatherings are frequent and important – as demonstrated in the novel through the celebration of family birthdays and events such as 'Tomato Day'. Children are raised to remain close to their families and are expected to incorporate their relatives into their new family when they grow up and marry.

Food also plays a central role in Italian culture, and is typically linked to family. Like family connections, food provides nourishment and connection to heritage, with different regions having different customs and traditions centred around food.

Religion is similarly important to Italian life, with the Pope and the Vatican (which governs the Catholic Church) located in Rome, and the majority of Italians identifying as Roman Catholic. While the number of practising Roman Catholics has declined over the last few decades, the Church still provides the moral framework within which many people live, with strict expectations regarding marriage, sex, mourning and divorce. While the stigma around some of these has lessened in recent years, attitudes regarding expected and appropriate behaviours, and judgement of those who do not adhere, can clearly be seen in the novel.

Sydney in the 1990s

Sydney was considerably smaller than it is today, with the 1990 population being 3.5 million, compared to over 5.3 million in 2021. The inner suburbs, where most of the action of the novel occurs, had yet to experience gentrification, and Glebe was a relatively cheap suburb (away from the waterfront), with a mixed population demographic. Leichardt was known for its large Italian population, having been a key destination for migrant settlement since 1947. Compared to some of the other suburbs referenced in the novel, Redfern had a notably lower socioeconomic level, and in the 1990s grew to be considered one of the most dangerous suburbs of inner Sydney, rife with drugs, crime and violence.

GENRE, STRUCTURE & LANGUAGE

Genre

Looking for Alibrandi fits very clearly into the category of young adult fiction, with the novel targeting a readership similar in age to a number of its main characters. Like many other titles that fall into this category, such as *The Fault in Our Stars* and *The Hunger Games*, the action is narrated in the first person from the protagonist's point of view, which allows greater scope for self-reflection. This genre of writing typically follows a young person navigating the challenge of developing their individual identity and establishing their place in the adult world.

While *Looking for Alibrandi* only focuses on one year of its protagonist's life, it can certainly be described as a **coming-of-age novel**, because of the 'growing up' that Josie does within that time period. Marchetta focuses on a number of key rites of passage, such as leaving school, the prospect of first sexual experiences and considering one's career path, while layering on additional emotional challenges such as cultural identity and an absent father figure.

The text could also be described as a **bildungsroman**, an 'education novel' that has a greater focus on a protagonist's growth in maturity and explores their psychological and moral development. Often this is the result of a life-changing event or emotional challenge. Bildungsromans often feature a protagonist who is questioning themselves, an element of their life or their place in the world, and this drives them to seek answers through life experience or knowledge. Throughout *Looking for Alibrandi*, Marchetta depicts Josie's psychological and emotional growth, as she seeks to establish her identity and determine how she fits into contemporary Australian society. Her battles with elements of gender, culture, social class, national identity and family all play significant roles in the novel, and Josie must reconcile herself with all of these aspects to achieve her goal of 'finding' herself.

Structure

'In medias res' is a Latin term meaning 'into the middle of things' and refers to starting a story in the middle of the action. The backstory is then filled in as the story progresses, through the use of flashbacks or description. Marchetta employs this as a strategy to 'hook' readers from the beginning, and to immerse them in the world of the narrative. We first meet Josie in a state of panic, confused about 'the multiple choice options which lay on [the] desk in front of [her]' (p.1). This introduction instantly locates the action in the classroom, which is accurate, but this apparently serious situation is subsequently undercut by the revelation that the quiz is in *Hot Pants* magazine.

Language

Narrative viewpoint

Looking for Alibrandi is similar to many other novels aimed at young adults in that it uses the first-person narrative voice. Josie's journey is presented in her own voice, and this allows Marchetta to explore the personal emotional impact on Josie of the events that occur. The novel follows Josie as she attempts to 'find herself' and develop her own sense of place in an unfamiliar world. We, as readers, are afforded access to her inner thoughts, feelings and reflections on the people she interacts with and the experiences she has.

First-person narratives should be approached with a degree of scepticism and an awareness that a biased view of events is being presented. In contrast to texts with a third-person omniscient narrator, which are able to present events from multiple perspectives, a first-person narrative shapes readers' view of events through the lens of only one character. To encourage readers' scepticism, Marchetta portrays Josie as frequently irrational and quite selfish in her reactions to situations, positioning readers to reflect on her behaviour and respond critically at times. As the novel tracks the gradual emotional development of its main character, readers are able to appreciate Josie's increasing ability to approach situations with maturity.

Slang and dialect

The experience of being caught between two worlds or cultures is explored extensively within the novel, with Marchetta highlighting the dislocation Josie feels as an Australian of Italian heritage. Note how she incorporates a combination of Australian and Italian phrases, cultural references and terminology to evoke the contrast in experience and influence. Even names are used differently at times, with the protagonist being referred to as 'Jozzie' and 'Giuseppina' when with her grandmother or extended family, illustrating a change in how she is viewed.

The use of Italian phrases and broken English is particularly important in relation to the relationship between Katia and Josie, as it helps to illustrate the differences in their lived experiences and the communication gap that exists between them at times. Marchetta portrays Katia as not always being able to convey her thoughts or feelings with clarity and precision, which then contributes to the misunderstanding and conflict between her and Josie.

The significance of the title

As a novel focused on its protagonist's exploration of her identity, the title seems initially straightforward – Josie is trying to find herself. Consider, however, that the title uses her family name, rather than her forename – the novel is not called 'Looking for Josephine'. This encourages readers to consider the wider implications of the novel: that this is a story of different generations within a family searching for their identity, rather than being solely focused on the main character. There is also a level of irony in the title, given the revelation that Christina is not Francesco's daughter and, as Josie chooses to take her father's surname at the end of the novel, the 'search' for Alibrandi is ultimately futile, given that no one in the text is actually an Alibrandi by blood.

CHAPTER-BY-CHAPTER ANALYSIS

Chapter 1 (pp.1–17)

Summary: *Josie introduces herself, her school and her family situation, focusing on the disconnect she feels in all aspects of her life as a seventeen-year-old in the inner suburbs of Sydney in the early 1990s.*

The novel begins in the middle of the action (in medias res), and the playfulness of Marchetta's writing is apparent immediately. Josie is agonising over a series of multiple-choice options within a school setting; readers are led to believe that she is completing a test of significance, given that getting an answer wrong 'would be too devastating for [her] sense of being' (p.1). However, it is swiftly revealed that the 'test' in question is in *Hot Pants* magazine, and relates to being a good friend. This humorous opening establishes the tone for the rest of the novel, where serious and frivolous events are blended, and the action is presented in the conversational style of the teenage narrator.

Josie then provides an extensive introduction to herself, in a style reminiscent of a film voice-over. She outlines her school life, her relationship with her mother and her illegitimacy. These elements are all sources of concern for Josie in different ways and contribute to her sense of disconnect. Marchetta includes particular focus on her Italian heritage here, in order to set up the cultural conflict that Josie battles throughout the novel. The social divides within Sydney are touched upon also, as Josie notes that people like her 'didn't belong in the eastern and northern suburbs' (p.8).

Key point

Josie tends to focus on what she lacks or is missing, before acknowledging the positive, as in her description of their living room (p.10). This highlights that – at this stage of the novel at least – she is more concerned with outward appearance than anything else.

The chapter concludes with the revelation that Michael Andretti, Josie's absent father, is back in Sydney. Josie is conflicted about this news, as she oscillates from 'explod[ing] angrily' (p.16) to 'trying to act uninterested' (p.17).

Key vocabulary

At Seventeen: Grammy-award-winning 1975 song by Janis Ian about the challenges of being a teenage girl and feeling disconnected and not fitting in.

Lost in Space: 1960s American television show about a family stuck in outer space.

Mario Lanza: Italian-American singer and actor popular in the 1940s and 1950s.

Tottenham: Tottenham Hotspur, also known as Spurs; an English soccer team based in London.

Q What are your first impressions of Josie?

Q What are Josie's major concerns with her life? Do you think these will change as the novel progresses?

Chapter 2 (pp.18–32)

Summary: *Josie introduces her friends; they attend the annual 'Have a Say Day' at Martin Place, where Josie has to make a speech; she chats with Jacob Coote, captain of Cook High, who surprises everyone with a passionate speech.*

Friendship is the central theme in this chapter, which focuses on the relationship Josie has with her peers. Her insecurity, even with her close friends, is illustrated right from the beginning, as she articulates her conflicted feelings about the return of her father but notes that she 'couldn't tell [her] friends about it yet' (p.18). This ties in with her feelings that her friendship group only exists because they don't fit in anywhere else.

At this stage of the novel, Josie is very focused on appearances. She observes that other friendship groups in the school are 'clone groups' with members who 'all look similar' (p.18), and the fact her group is different is presented as a failing on their part. This tendency to judge people by their outward appearance is present later in the chapter when she encounters Jacob Coote and is astounded by the passion with which he speaks. Her prejudice is highlighted by Lee, who tells her 'you still think you're better than the average person' (p.31), and acknowledged by Josie herself, who admits that she wants to belong to 'the world of sleek haircuts and upper-class privileges' and 'be accepted by someone other than the underdog' (p.32).

Aside from Jacob Coote, who represents the working-class public-school students, we are also introduced to Ivy Lloyd, who represents the opposite. Portrayed as Josie's nemesis for much of the novel, 'Poison Ivy' is everything Josie aspires to be, and everything she feels she is denied.

Key vocabulary

Bolero: a cropped jacket or cardigan.

Hinch: a current affairs show hosted by Derryn Hinch that ran from 1987 to 1994.

Valiant: a car manufactured by Chrysler.

Q What indications are there in this chapter that Josie is attracted to Jacob? How do appearances and preconceived ideas affect her view of him?

Chapter 3 (pp.33–40)

Summary: *Josie visits Nonna after school and meets Michael Andretti for the first time.*

This chapter focuses on Josie's relationship with Nonna (grandmother) Katia, and more broadly on intergenerational relationships and conflict.

The expectations that people have of others is also explored, along with how people react when others fail to meet those expectations.

Katia's expectations of her daughter and granddaughter are influenced by her Italian upbringing, with outward appearance and respect towards one's elders holding great significance. Katia is, as Josie notes, 'always worrying about what other people think' and 'always talking about other people' (p.37), and Josie is critical of this attitude where everyone is scrutinised for their behaviour and whether they adhere to some unwritten list of 'ridiculous rules and regulations' (p.40). There is, however, an irony in Josie's reaction during her first encounter with Michael, as he turns out to be nothing like she expected, with Josie listing all the things 'he wasn't' (p.38).

Josie feels trapped by the conflicting expectations of being both Australian and Italian. While she declares her determination to 'run one day ... to be free and think for [her]self' (p.40), she acknowledges that she is not entirely in control of her choices and can only do things 'if [her] society will let [her]' (p.40).

Key vocabulary

Flibbertigibbet: a talkative person.

Q Is Josie's behaviour towards Nonna fair here? Why / why not? Consider the argument from both perspectives.

Chapter 4 (pp.41–50)

Summary: *The debating season begins, enabling Josie to spend time with John Barton; they chat, and John reveals his fears about the future that has been mapped out for him.*

John Barton is introduced in glowing terms, with Josie portraying him as perfect in every way, except for him not being attracted to her. He is presented as having it all – good looks, brains, wealth, connections and popularity – and on a social and material level he has everything Josie yearns for.

Marchetta challenges the superficiality of Josie's view of John by depicting him as a deeply troubled young man who feels just as restricted as Josie. Both are trapped by familial expectations, albeit of a different nature, and both view the other as 'so in control' (p.46), illustrating how one's perception of oneself can be markedly different from others' perceptions. While Josie views John's wealth and status as enviable and something to aspire to, for him it is a burden that prevents him from having any control over his life and future. At this stage in the novel, Josie is too self-focused to notice the warning signs about John's emotional state, only observing 'a darkness in his eyes' and that his behaviour is 'a bit freaky' (p.46).

Q What are the different pressures on John and Josie?

Chapter 5 (pp.51–63)

Summary: *Josie and her friends attend the regional dance, which is also attended by students from Cook High and St. Anthony's; Josie dances with Jacob, and he later gives her a lift home on his motorbike.*

The regional dance brings together four different schools, providing the opportunity for the different characters in the novel to come together socially. The pre-dance discussions around clothing highlight the different views within the Alibrandi family about appropriate attire, again reinforcing that appearance is intrinsically linked to judgement. Josie, while dismissing the attitudes of her mother and grandmother, still places significant value on appearance, as each of the other characters is introduced with a detailed description of their hair and outfit.

While Jacob's outward appearance continues to be rough and ready, an image that is further reinforced by his motorbike riding, Marchetta hints that there is sensitivity and depth underneath his brash exterior. Jacob challenges Josie's judgement of him, reminding her that she doesn't 'know what [he] is all about' (p.55), before speaking candidly about his emotional journey following the death of his mother. Jacob is, however, also guilty of judging on appearances, deeming John to be 'the type of guy who goes to uni and decides to be gay because it's trendy' (p.58).

Key point

Marchetta depicts almost every character making snap judgements about others at some point during the novel, not just Josie. Consider how the author uses this to highlight the prevalence of judgement and prejudice in society, and challenges readers to consider their own behaviour towards others.

Q How do the chosen outfits of each of the characters described in the chapter reflect their different personalities?

Chapter 6 (pp.64–72)

Summary: *Josie attends a family barbecue at her grandmother's house; Michael is also present, and Josie confronts him; Katia comes to the realisation that Michael is Josie's father.*

Michael, Christina and Josie watch each other from a distance during the barbecue, before Christina and Michael have a heated discussion about Josie, which she eavesdrops on. Michael is clearly grappling with the recent revelation that he has a daughter. He fluctuates between being combative and attempting to do what he perceives to be the right thing: offering to provide financial support.

Following the discussion between Christina and Michael, Josie confronts Michael herself. Theirs is a more emotionally charged conversation, with Josie's emotional immaturity clearly displayed in her angry but confused attack on Michael. She knows she wants to challenge him and that she's angry, but her inability to think past that results in their conversation lacking direction and intent. They do, however, resolve to keep out of each other's lives.

Later that evening, Christina and Josie discuss their dreams. Note the simplicity and superficiality in Josie's dream 'of being successful and of falling in love with someone with money' (p.71), highlighting that, at this point, her aspirations are still very materialistic. Contrast this with Christina's recollection of her dream at seventeen, 'of marrying a man who didn't necessarily have to have money, but who would take care of me' (p.72). These dreams highlight some of the things absent in their respective childhoods – Christina having grown up in a house with little love and affection, and Josie lacking the financial stability experienced by many of her friends.

Q As readers, how are we positioned to view Michael at this point in the novel?

Q Why does Marchetta include Christina's dreams here as well? Consider the later revelations in the novel to help you answer this.

Chapter 7 (pp.73–9)

Summary: *Josie goes to stay overnight with Nonna, who tells her stories about her youth and her migration to Australia.*

With Josie forced to stay overnight with her, Katia relates stories of her youth to her granddaughter. Katia recalls her marriage as a seventeen-year-old, and her voyage to Australia. Her account focuses on the challenges that migrants of the time faced, going to an unknown country, with no real prospect of ever seeing their family again. The contrast in cultures is highlighted, along with the poverty in which new migrants lived.

Pondering the stories, Josie reflects on the challenges faced by the previous generations of her family and shows signs of realising that her life may not be as bad as she thinks. While the chapter is dominated by Katia's recollections, the occasional interjections by Josie – e.g. 'Such self-sacrifice is very hard for me to understand' (p.76) – suggest that she is beginning to look outside of herself and appreciate the experiences of others.

Key vocabulary

Glory box: a box in which a young woman stores things in preparation for her marriage.

Paese: an Italian word meaning either country or village.

Zingara: an Italian word meaning a 'gypsy' woman.

Q Stories of Nonna's past appear at intervals throughout the novel. Why might Marchetta have placed this particular story here? Consider the conclusion of the previous chapter.

Chapter 8 (pp.80–90)

Summary: *Josie hits Carly Bishop in the face with her science book; Josie calls Michael to help get her out of her predicament.*

Josie calls out Carly Bishop, a part-time model who belongs to the 'beautiful people' (p.80) at St. Martha's, for using a racist epithet. This results in a verbal stoush between them, which culminates in Josie hitting Carly in the face with her science book after she refers to both Josie's ethnicity and her illegitimacy. The casual racism of the Anglocentric elements of Australian society is highlighted, along with Josie's sensitivity about where she fits in.

When threatened with legal action by Carly's father, who is a television presenter, Josie calls Michael to help extricate her from the situation. With no real expectation that he will come to her rescue, Josie anticipates being expelled. Michael does, however, come to the school, and resolves the situation. The conversation between Michael and Josie (pp.86–8) positions him as frank and no-nonsense, forcing Josie to articulate the reasons for her actions and to take a more adult approach.

Despite receiving punishment for her actions, Josie revels in the 'great feeling' of 'walking alongside [her] father' (p.90), pointing to the potential for a relationship between them.

Key vocabulary

Doctor Kildare: a famous, fictional, television doctor from the 1960s.

Q Why is Josie reluctant to tell Michael the truth about why she hit Carly?

Chapter 9 (pp.91–9)

Summary: *Sister Louise checks in on Josie; Katia confronts Christina about Michael being Josie's father; Josie and Christina argue about Christina going on a date with a colleague.*

This chapter focuses on roles, responsibilities and appearances. It begins with Sister Louise checking in on Josie, to make sure she's coping with all the changes in her life. Josie reflects on how nuns are more worldly than they're usually perceived to be, and Sister Louise reveals that she rode a motorbike as a teenager, thus contradicting the perception Josie has of her.

The bulk of the chapter focuses on the relationships between mothers and daughters in the Alibrandi family. Katia berates Christina for 'disgrac[ing her] with Pia Maria Andretti's son' (p.96), highlighting the interconnected nature of Italian life, and then further criticises her for 'neglecting' Josie and going on a date with Paul Presilio (p.95). Christina, for the first time, is presented as an independent woman, with desires of her own, and she stands up to both her mother and her daughter.

Key vocabulary

Habit: the clothing worn by nuns, or those in a religious order.

The Sound of Music: a 1965 film featuring nuns and starring Julie Andrews.

Wimple: the head covering worn by nuns.

Q What is the deeper meaning of Katia's comment, 'I understand, Christina, more than you think I do' (p.97)?

Chapter 10 (pp.100–8)

Summary: *Josie and Anna are attacked while working at McDonald's, and are saved by Jacob; Jacob asks Josie out, but baulks at her expectation that he should meet her mother first.*

Josie outlines the challenges of her job at McDonald's, most notably that 'it's the hang-out for every hood in the inner west and inner city' (p.100). One night after their shift Josie and Anna are attacked by Greg Sims (a bully and low-life who used to live next door to Josie) and his friends. Josie recounts the abuse she and her mother endured from the Sims family, and the name-calling she was subjected to by Greg. Here, the attack is much worse, with Greg and his cronies physically attacking Josie and Anna, and threatening them sexually, before Jacob intervenes. Greg makes assumptions that Josie will be 'like her mother' (p.104), referring to the cyclical nature of life that is touched on by several characters in the text.

Jacob then drives Josie home and asks her out, but they hit a hurdle when she states that this would require him to meet her mother. The clash in expectations resulting from their different cultural backgrounds presents a potential stumbling block for the relationship, but ultimately Jacob agrees to meet Christina, and Josie agrees that she'll ask if she can go out with him.

Chapter 11 (pp.109–13)

Summary: *Josie and Christina reconcile; Josie asks her mother for permission to go out with Jacob.*

Josie apologises for her reaction to her mother dating, showing a self-awareness that has been hitherto hidden. She asks for permission to go to the cinema with Jacob, which Christina is reticent about because she doesn't know him. They discuss Christina's date, and talk openly about sex, with the suggestion that the AIDS epidemic has made sex and contraception much less of a taboo subject.

Key vocabulary

Romper Room: an American television show aimed at pre-school children.

Q Is Josie genuine in her apology to Christina, or is she only doing it because she wants to go out with Jacob? Provide reasons for your answer.

Chapter 12 (pp.114–18)

Summary: *Josie asks Nonna to show her her photographs, which include one of Marcus Sandford.*

Nonna Katia relates the story of her early years in Australia, and the isolation that she experienced. The challenges of being far away from one's family are explored, and Katia tells of her friendship with the Australian Marcus Sandford, with Marchetta providing subtle hints that there was more to the relationship than Katia reveals here. Josie begins to appreciate the life that she has, and how her challenges are nothing in comparison to those faced by previous generations of her family.

Chapter 13 (pp.119–31)

Summary: *Josie goes on a date with Jacob, which is an unmitigated disaster; she leaves, and ends up having dinner with Michael.*

The night of Josie's date with Jacob arrives; she has spent considerable time and money preparing, and telling Christina repeatedly about all of his good qualities. Jacob arrives, unshaven, wearing torn and scruffy clothes, and barely acknowledges Christina. Josie is furious with him and they argue repeatedly. At the cinema they cannot agree on a film, and their disagreement turns nasty, with Jacob referring to Josie's ethnicity.

After storming off, Josie is trailed by a car, which fortunately turns out to be Michael. They go for pizza and begin to get to know each other. Michael confesses his misgivings about getting to know Josie, admitting he doesn't necessarily want to be a father, and that he may not have behaved any differently had he known Christina had not had an abortion.

Key vocabulary

Bill Collins: Australian film critic.

Q How does the argument with Jacob highlight some of the hypocrisy in Josie's attitude regarding cultural identity?

Chapter 14 (pp.132–8)

Summary: *Josie bumps into John, who reveals his negative thoughts about life.*

Josie meets John and they go for coffee, but John is a different person from the one Josie is used to. He is extremely negative about everything, particularly his relationship with his father, continuing with his previously expressed concerns about not wanting to follow the path his father has determined for him. While Josie has made progress over the course of the novel in becoming less self-absorbed, she fails to realise the extent of John's depression, and wishes she was somewhere else and notes that she 'wasn't as attracted to him as [she] used to be' (p.132). They exchange letters about how they're feeling, with the intention of opening them after their HSC is over.

Josie's developing comfort in her identity is illustrated by her ability to ignore Sera baiting her about her illegitimacy. Her immaturity, however, is still evident as she still aspires to 'be rich and influential' and 'to flaunt [her] status' (p.138), demonstrating that she has yet to grasp what is important in life.

Key vocabulary

Jimmy Swaggart: American televangelist (a preacher who appears on television).

The Cockroaches: an Australian band from the 1980s.

Chapter 15 (pp.139–48)

Summary: *Josie and her friends hang out at a cafe popular with teenagers discussing their career aspirations; Jacob and Josie make up after their argument.*

While hanging out at Harley's, the friends discuss their career aspirations and the options available to them. The restrictions imposed by class and social divisions are highlighted by Lee, who believes that everyone's future is essentially governed by their family, meaning that 'we all end up where we started', in contrast to Josie's view that 'we're masters of our own destiny' (p.144). This illustrates something of a change in Josie, who has struggled with the burden of her past throughout the novel, but now believes she has some control over her life.

After Lee leaves, Josie chats to Jacob at the bus stop. They kiss, and agree to skip school on Friday to hang out. Jacob apologises for the things he said. Despite previously acknowledging to herself that she was also in the wrong as she'd 'had too many expectations' and had 'wanted [Jacob] to be what [she] wanted and not what he was' (p.135), Josie doesn't apologise to Jacob for her behaviour.

Q What is the significance of Lee's view on how life works, particularly as it appears so soon after revelation of John's depressed attitude?

Chapter 16 (pp.149–55)

Summary: *Josie wags (skips) school to be with Jacob.*

Josie meets Jacob and they spend the day in Manly. She describes his physical appearance and personality in greater detail than before, highlighting the contrast between his outward appearance and his inner sensitivity. Josie is beginning to realise that there is more to most people than initial appearances indicate.

They discuss their families, and their markedly different behavioural conventions. Despite criticising the cultural mores she has been subject to throughout the novel, it is notable that Josie's first response to Jacob telling her about his father's girlfriend Eileen staying over is 'are they engaged?' (p.151), suggesting that these expectations are still ingrained in her.

There is, however, the suggestion that Josie is beginning to find peace with her Italian heritage, as she notes that 'you can't hate what you're part of' (p.152) – a much calmer response to culture than at other times in the novel. Her increased maturity is also illustrated at the end of the chapter when she acknowledges her feelings for Jacob. Though part of her wants 'to be in love with John Barton and have people look upon [her] with envy', she realises that 'things don't turn out the way you want them to' and that this can sometimes be for the better (p.155).

Key vocabulary

Mills and Boon: a publisher that specialises in romantic fiction.

Chapter 17 (pp.156–64)

Summary: *Josie goes to Adelaide with Michael during the mid-year holidays; she gets to know him better and meets her extended family.*

This chapter focuses on the development of relationships, with a strong emphasis on the importance of getting to know people, and how that influences the relationship that follows.

While driving to Adelaide, Michael reveals that he has chatted with Jacob, which surprises Josie. This leads to a discussion about Michael and Christina's relationship when they were teenagers, and the challenges they faced, which are not dissimilar to those Josie has related. With the benefit of hindsight, Michael can acknowledge their unpreparedness for a sexual relationship, and his reflection of this is an interesting counterpoint to Josie and Jacob's burgeoning romance. The growing intensity between Josie and Jacob is emphasised by him telling her to 'never to go anywhere again because he'd missed [her]' while she was in Adelaide (p.164).

Josie meets and spends time with her paternal aunt, cousins and grandparents. There is some stiltedness, which Josie accepts. She displays a level of maturity in recognising the difficulty her new grandparents have in coming to terms with her existence, which indicates the growth she has undergone since the beginning of the novel.

Key vocabulary

Ansett: an Australian airline that no longer exists.

Chapter 18 (pp.165–70)

Summary: *Josie argues with Poison Ivy about her background; Jacob gets a car.*

While waiting for their regular meeting with Sister Louise, Poison Ivy makes a remark about 'new Australians' (p.165) to Josie, resulting in an argument. The term, along with the word 'ethnic', highlights the casual racism towards Australians of European background that was prevalent at the time, and illustrates the challenges that Josie faces in trying to determine where she fits in. As an Australian-born child of two Australian-born parents, she feels quite distant from her Italian heritage, and yet it is used to differentiate her from others in society.

Jacob surprises Josie with a car, which he has been fixing up in his spare time. They joke about their future together but acknowledge the differences in their aspirations and strengths.

Q What does the conversation between Jacob and Josie on page 169 suggest about their relationship?

Chapter 19 (pp.171–5)

Summary: *Josie's family gathers to make pasta sauce, an event Josie calls 'Tomato Day'.*

The whole of Josie's family is gathered at Nonna Katia's house to make pasta sauce. Josie and her cousin Robert are mortified by this annual event and cannot understand why they can't buy sauce at a supermarket.

The event provides an opportunity for a family get-together, and Katia and Zia Patrizia reminisce about their early years in Queensland and the hardships they faced. It is revealed that Marcus Sandford helped the women after their husbands had been interned because of Italy being a German ally during the war. Patrizia recalls the death of her son, who drowned in a creek and was found by Marcus Sandford.

Despite Josie's apparent resentment of Tomato Day at the beginning of the chapter, things end on a relatively positive note, as she recognises that tradition is intrinsic to identity, even if at this point she still wishes she could escape it.

Key vocabulary

Franklin's: a supermarket chain.

Gioia: Italian word meaning joy.

Q Consider the placing of this chapter directly after Ivy and Josie's argument about the term 'new Australians'. What does this chapter suggest about Australian attitudes to Italian migrants?

Chapter 20 (pp.176–85)

Summary: *Josie and her friend skip the annual St. Martha's walk-a-thon in an attempt to see a celebrity; after being caught by television cameras, Josie is reprimanded by Sister Louise about her lack of responsibility.*

While waiting for the annual charity walk-a-thon to begin, Sera reveals that an American singer is staying at a nearby hotel. The friends decide to skip the walk-a-thon and go to the hotel in search of him. Josie has misgivings from the beginning, as she is meant to be at the back of the group, helping to keep the younger students safe. The girls fail to find the celebrity, but they do inadvertently appear on television after being caught by cameras filming the Premier.

The next day, the four girls are severely reprimanded for their behaviour by Sister Louise, who emphasises that her trust in them has been broken. Sister Louise is particularly disgusted in Josie, who she calls 'a sheep' (p.181) for following her friends rather than showing the leadership her position requires; she compares her to Ivy Lloyd, who she describes as 'responsible from the moment she walks into this school till the moment she walks out' (p.182). Sister Louise also reveals that Josie was actually voted school captain, but that she made the decision to award the position to Ivy because of questions around Josie's behaviour. Josie is forced to look critically at herself, and to realise that not only was her behaviour wrong, but that her perception of how others see her is also wrong.

Key vocabulary

Molly Meldrum: an Australian music presenter.

Q Why does Josie 'think that [her] emancipation began at that moment' (p.185)? How do the events of this chapter help to free her?

Chapter 21 (pp.186–93)

Summary: *Josie goes to see* Macbeth *at the cinema with John; Jacob is there and is jealous.*

As agreed in Chapter 4, Josie and John go to the cinema to see *Macbeth*, a text they are both studying at school. John is more upbeat than when they last met and is dismissive of his previous negativity. There is, however, a hint that all is still not well, as he changes the subject quickly after Josie starts discussing 'careers and school marks' (p.187).

At the cinema, Josie spots Jacob glaring at them. It is clear that Josie knows she has behaved poorly, as her 'heart stopped' and she speaks to him 'in a small voice' (p.187), even though she acts as though nothing is wrong. There is some macho posturing between the two boys, before Jacob points out the hypocrisy in Josie's behaviour by asking how she'd feel if he went to the cinema alone with a female friend. As Jacob points out, Josie goes 'about whinging and wailing about the way people treat [her], but [she] never think[s] about the way [she] treat[s] people' (p.191). While they do make up by the end of the chapter, the incident highlights Josie's double standards, including how she is critical of those who make assumptions about her, but is equally guilty of making them about others.

Chapter 22 (pp.194–8)

Summary: *Josie and Christina spend a day together treating themselves and discussing life.*

Having a 'splurge' in Sydney provides Josie and Christina with an opportunity to spend time together and chat. Christina has been noticeably absent from the events of the novel, having not appeared since Chapter 13. This reflects the changing nature of Josie's relationships – previously her main close relationship was with her mother, but the appearance of Michael and her dating of Jacob has meant that she now has other significant people in her life.

Christina talks honestly about the challenges of her teenage relationship with Michael, and the pain he caused her. She also speaks openly about her difficult relationship with her father, and how he treated her when she became pregnant. The later revelation of her parentage is foreshadowed here, when Christina notes, 'I don't think he really loved me and I always wondered why. I don't think he loved Nonna either … It was as if she owed him something, but I can't understand what' (p.196).

Key vocabulary

Jane Fonda: an American actress who had a popular home workout video series in the 1980s.

Q Although Josie is on the cusp of adulthood, at times she still thinks in a childlike way. What examples of this are there in this chapter?

Chapter 23 (pp.199–202)

Summary: *Nonna Katia and Josie discuss the past, including Katia's move to Sydney.*

Josie's relationship with Nonna continues to improve, as they discuss more of the past. Katia reveals more about her early years in Australia, and how she came to move to, and settle in, Sydney. She confesses that she did see Marcus Sandford again, and that he was in love with her.

Katia outlines more of the challenges faced by migrant women in the mid-twentieth century, where gossip could kill and women were married under false pretences. This is also a foreshadowing of sorts, given Francesco's later revelation of his impotence. Following these stories, Josie reflects on multiculturalism more broadly, and the changes in the Australian demographic. Her point, sadly, seems to be that a lot has remained the same since the 1950s, and there is still a long way to go.

Q Consider the changes that have occurred in Australia since *Looking for Alibrandi* was published (in 1992). Are the issues raised by Josie in this chapter still prevalent today?

Chapter 24 (pp.203–14)

Summary: *Jacob meets Josie after school and is upset that she won't introduce him to Nonna Katia; after their fight, Josie goes to Jacob's home in Redfern and meets his father.*

Jacob is upset that Josie does not want to introduce him to her Nonna, believing it indicates that Josie is ashamed of him. He challenges her to do as she pleases, rather than adhering to rules that she hasn't made.

The next day, Josie goes to Redfern to visit Jacob. She is initially nervous and feels self-conscious but seeing girls like her sitting and chatting helps her feel more comfortable, and suggests that she is beginning to realise that people are people, no matter where you go. Jacob is resistant to her visit, turning her words around on her and suggesting that his father wouldn't approve of him 'going out with a non-Australian' (p.208). While Josie dismisses this, her inability to see things from Jacob's perspective is clear.

After meeting Jacob's father, Josie joins Jacob in his bedroom, and things get physical between them. Josie is comfortable with this progression in their relationship to a point but stops things when she is concerned that they might have sex. Their different attitudes to sex are clear but they are able to talk things through, which is a step forward in their relationship.

Key vocabulary

Botch: to stuff up; to make a mess of.

Chapter 25 (pp.215–19)

Summary: *At Christina's birthday party, Josie realises Marcus Sandford is Christina's father, and she later confronts Nonna about this.*

With Christina's birthday falling on 1 October, at her birthday party the family tease her about being 'conceived on New Years Day' (p.215) or within the Christmas period. When Zia Patrizia points out that Christina was born during Francesco and Katia's first year in Sydney, Josie realises that her grandfather was not with her grandmother during the time that Christina was conceived. Joining the dots between the information Nonna has given her during their discussions, Josie suddenly realises that Marcus Sandford is Christina's real father, and this revelation changes everything.

Josie stays after everyone else has left and confronts her grandmother angrily, calling her 'a liar' (p.216) and attacking her for her hypocritical treatment of Christina. Josie criticises Katia for warning her and her mother against Australians and their different way of life and forcing them to be so aware of their behaviour and what others think, when all the while she has behaved in a far worse way.

After leaving, Josie reflects on this new information about the reality of her heritage. Her speculation about what her family's life would have been like as Sandfords illustrates her perception that much of her sense of disconnection is related to her Italian heritage; however, she does show acceptance of her background, as her final desire in the chapter is to be 'an insignificant Italian in a normal Italian family' (p.219).

Chapter 26 (pp.220–6)

Summary: *Josie reconciles with Nonna, who shares the story of her relationship with Marcus Sandford.*

Josie's developing maturity is further displayed here as her anger at Katia subsides quickly, and she reveals she no longer cares about what people are saying behind her back. She is, as she notes, 'beginning to feel free' (p.221).

Josie voluntarily visits Katia and asks to hear her side of the story. Katia describes her relationship with Marcus Sandford, and how both cultural and social expectations meant that they could never be together. There are clear similarities with some of the prejudice that Josie has encountered, but Katia emphasises that the pressures on her were even greater as divorce was simply not an option, especially not within the small Italian community. Katia reveals Francesco's deception of her, as he knew he was unable to father children, and outlines the awful compromise that they reach, where he agrees to raise Christina as his own, and Katia keeps her infidelity secret. This compromise results in a socially acceptable facade of appropriateness, but Katia highlights the emotional distance in their relationship and how she was powerless to help Christina when she became pregnant because of the power her husband held over her.

Q How does this chapter illustrate that Josie is 'beginning to feel free'?

Chapter 27 (pp.227–30)

Summary: *Josie goes to watch her cousin's rugby grand final and catches up with John.*

On the surface, this is a relatively upbeat chapter, providing some light relief after the revelations of the previous chapters. There are, however, a number of red flags in the dialogue between John and Josie that foreshadow John's impending suicide.

John is markedly different from previous encounters, behaving in an upbeat and outgoing way. He has a confidence about his level of control over the future, stating that 'the future is mine, to do whatever I want with it' (p.229), but, heartbreakingly, it transpires that he views his only way of exercising this control is by ending his life.

This a chapter that reads very differently after the first reading. Initially it seeks to trick the reader, suggesting that things are positive for both John and Josie, making the events of the next chapter even more shocking. On subsequent readings, however, with the knowledge of what happens, it is full of awful irony, with Josie using typically dramatic teenage language when she talks of 'surviv[ing] the HSC' and 'just want[ing] it to be over' (p.229), while John apparently talks positively about the future.

Q What signs are there in this chapter that John has already made his decision to end his life? Identify quotes that indicate this.

Chapter 28 (pp.231–40)

Summary: *John's suicide is revealed, and its impact on several characters is explored.*

The chapter opens in a run-of-the-mill fashion, presenting the day as a very ordinary one. This makes the revelation of John's death a significant surprise, positioning readers to share Josie's shock and confusion. The emotional rollercoaster that Josie experiences in the immediate aftermath of John's death and the following few days as she works through her grief is reflected in the writing style in this chapter. Initially, Josie's reaction is disbelief, and she says little, in contrast with her usual chatty behaviour. The prose focuses on her physical response, highlighting her initial inability to process the news mentally. As the chapter progresses, she becomes more verbose, conveying her anger about John's suicide to Michael, and her youth is emphasised by her demand of Michael, 'You're an adult, tell me', and her reference to Christina as 'Mummy' rather than 'Mama' (p.235). There is a dream-like quality to the chapter, which covers an unspecified period of time from the revelation of John's death until sometime after the funeral, reflecting the unreality that can be experienced after the sudden loss of a loved one. Josie jumps from recounting one event to another, without the clear, logical flow that has been present elsewhere.

Through the reactions of other characters, particularly Jacob – who wasn't close to John – Marchetta conveys the wider impact of the event, and the different ways that people respond to death. Given John's wealth, intelligence and privilege, his death is even more of a surprise, with Jacob asking, 'What have the rest of us got to look forward to if he had nothing?' (p.239); however, through this, Marchetta highlights that all levels of society experience pressures and challenges, and sometimes those who seem to have everything can be the most troubled.

Q Why does Josie tear up the poem that John has written?

Chapter 29 (pp.241–7)

Summary: *Josie attends her school speech night; afterwards, she goes out to dinner with Michael, who announces he's staying in Sydney and asks her to take his surname.*

Josie wins three awards at speech night, but Ivy is named dux. Josie's maturity is again evident, as she's able to acknowledge that Ivy 'deserved it more' (p.241). Josie's personal journey, coupled with the events of the year, have enabled her to look at things more rationally. Ivy and Josie share a conversation in the toilets, and the similarities between them are clear. They agree, at Josie's suggestion, to be friendly should they encounter each other at university.

After speech night, Michael takes Josie for dinner and reveals his pride in her. Notably, it is Michael, rather than Christina, who gets to celebrate with Josie after this key event, illustrating the progress in their relationship, and also Christina's willingness to make space for Michael, acknowledging that Josie has 'been all [hers] for so long and now [she's] his as well' (pp.246–7).

The growing importance of Josie to Michael is illustrated by his announcement that he's staying in Sydney and has bought a house in Balmain, which includes a bedroom specifically for Josie. He also asks her to take his surname, indicating his desire for there to be a formal connection between them. With Josie knowing her mother's real parentage, she has no 'real' connection to the Alibrandi name, but acknowledges it is her connection to Katia and Christina.

Q How has Michael changed since he was first introduced?

Chapter 30 (pp.248–52)

Summary: *Jacob breaks up with Josie.*

Jacob comes to Josie's house to break up with her. He believes that they are incompatible because of their different intelligence levels, and this makes him feel inadequate in comparison. After arguing initially about the cultural conflict between them, Jacob reveals the crisis of confidence he's been experiencing since being with Josie, and how it has made him question what he wants out of life. Instead of settling for a particular type of life, he wants 'to step outside [his] circle and look at the other options' (p.251). While Jacob acknowledges the role that Josie has played in giving him such aspirations, he recognises that finding himself is something he needs to do alone, showing a depth and maturity that Josie fails, understandably, to appreciate.

Q Josie has appeared more grown-up in recent chapters, but what evidence is there here of her emotional immaturity?

Chapter 31 (pp.253–7)

Summary: *Josie and her friends go out for pizza to celebrate the end of exams; they discuss sex and relationships.*

Josie and her friends discuss their relationships, with Anna admitting that she's been going out with Anton, and Lee revealing that she had sex the night before. This sparks more discussion about their varying attitudes to sex, with Josie continuing to wonder whether it would have made a difference to her relationship with Jacob if she had slept with him.

Q What are the four characters' different attitudes to sex? Has Josie's changed throughout the novel?

Chapter 32 (pp.258–61)

Summary: *Josie reflects on her year and realises that her emancipation has occurred.*

As she celebrates her eighteenth birthday, thus formally becoming an adult, Josie reflects on the events of the previous year and all the challenges and pressures she has faced. She addresses different aspects of her life – her perceived social disconnection, her illegitimacy, her cultural conflict, her family situation and her relationship with Jacob – and acknowledges that they are works in progress.

Key vocabulary

Sun City: a protest song written in opposition to racial segregation in South Africa, which was known as apartheid.

Q What does Josie mean when she says, 'Because finally I understood' (p.261)?

CHARACTERS & RELATIONSHIPS

Josephine Alibrandi

Key quotes

'I felt disadvantaged from the beginning.' (p.7)

'I dream of being successful and of falling in love with someone with money.' (p.71)

'But the important thing is that I know where my place in life is.' (p.258)

As indicated by the novel's title, Josie Alibrandi is a work in progress, a teenage girl uncertain of who she is or where she fits in. Conflicted by many aspects of her life – her illegitimacy, her Italian–Australian background, her appearance, her class and her social status – Josie spends the final year of high school trying to make peace with her identity. Ultimately, she is able to experience 'emancipation', and free herself from the labels that she, and others, have applied to her.

As she is both the protagonist and narrator of the novel, readers are positioned to follow Josie on her journey of self-discovery. This does not, however, mean that readers always support or agree with her behaviour. Josie is, at times, irrational and irresponsible, and she can be just as guilty of the judgemental behaviour she criticises others for.

At the beginning of the novel, Josie is presented as quite a superficial person who lacks self-awareness while also being very self-absorbed. She is highly critical of Nonna Katia's obsession with appearances and what others think, yet spends much of her time worrying about how she is perceived by others. Her aspirations, other than being a barrister, centre on wealth and status, as she yearns to be part of the moneyed elite populated by the likes of Ivy Lloyd and John Barton. She, erroneously as it transpires, believes that wealthy people have no concerns, and that their money and status make them immune to criticism or censure.

By the end of the novel, Josie has developed into a more mature young woman. Her relationships and experiences have pushed her to question her previous views, which are challenged by events such as John's suicide, her break-up with Jacob, her relationship with Michael, and Katia's revelation about Marcus Sandford. Josie realises that the only opinions that matter are those of the people who are important in her life, and the novel concludes with her contemplating global issues and family relationships, demonstrating progress from her previous desire for the superficial.

Relationships play a significant part in Josie's development. As the novel progresses, Josie's relationships and experiences provide her with different perspectives, and she begins to mature in her thinking. The introduction of Michael into her life provides her with a male point of view on things, as well as giving her insight into the person her mother was when she was young. By meeting her as an adult, Michael is also able to challenge Josie's way of thinking without the baggage of history. Her relationship with Jacob forces Josie to confront some of her own prejudices and judgements, and helps her to realise that some of the supposed rules she has to live by are actually self-imposed. Within her family, she develops a greater understanding of both Christina and Katia as actual people, with their own history and their own hopes and dreams, rather than seeing them merely as participants in her story.

Christina Alibrandi

Key quotes

'I am a young woman and I'm tired of being old.' (p.95)

'[F]or once someone found me interesting, not because I was Josie's mother or Katia's daughter, but because I was me …' (p.99)

'Josie, life is not a *Mills and Boon* book. People fall out of love. People disappoint other people and they find it very hard to forgive.' (p.198)

Christina is portrayed as a sympathetic character, a single mother doing her best, stuck between the expectations of her traditional mother and her teenage daughter. She is fiercely protective of Josie, as evidenced by her response to Michael's return and her concerns about him hurting her daughter. Christina's relationship with her own mother, Katia, is loving but fraught.

While the focus on Christina initially is as Josie's mother and Katia's daughter, as the novel progresses she is depicted as a woman in her own right. This encourages readers to consider the loss of identity women often experience when they become mothers, and is particularly relevant given that Christina is only in her mid-thirties. The return of Michael and her going on a date with Paul Presilio both provide opportunities to see Christina as an individual, rather than just in terms of her relationships. Christina's discussions with Josie, and Michael's recollections also, reveal a woman with hopes and aspirations that were curtailed by her pregnancy. While she is at pains to emphasise that she doesn't regret having her daughter, there is a sense of lost opportunities in Christina's life.

Katia Alibrandi

Key quotes

'I understand, Christina, more than you think I do.' (p.97)

'I did it because I had dreams just like you dream now. I was not always old.' (p.222)

'[Katia] hadn't lived life the way I'd thought. She hadn't stuck to rules and regulations. Hadn't worried about what other people thought every second of her life. She had taken chances. Broken rules.' (p.226)

As the oldest of the Alibrandi women, Nonna Katia presents a different perspective on expectations, relationships and migration. She represents an older generation whose beliefs are rooted in a different country and time, where traditions are a way of maintaining connection to things that have been left behind. Initially presented as a stubborn old woman who cares more about community gossip than the feelings of those she loves, Katia becomes an increasingly sympathetic figure as the story of her life is gradually revealed.

Trapped in an apparently loveless marriage with a man who couldn't father children and separated from the majority of her family by the prospect of a better life, Katia is shown to have endured a lot. It is not until the end of the novel when the full story of Christina's parentage is revealed that we are able to fully appreciate – and perhaps understand – Katia's behaviour. While she is undoubtably hypocritical, especially in how she behaves after Francesco's death when there is no longer the same requirement for her to follow expectations, she is a woman trapped between the traditions of the old and the freedom of the new.

Katia highlights the challenges faced by migrants, particularly women, of her generation who came to Australia. She reveals the tough conditions and isolation – both geographical and emotional – that they faced, often with no one to provide support and comfort. Having come from village life in Sicily, Katia found Australia to be a very different place, and adapting was a slow process. Through Katia's reflections on the difficulty of fitting in to life in Australia, readers are invited to consider what has actually changed since the early days of European migration, and how Australian societal attitudes to new migrants have – and haven't – progressed. There are, of course, similarities between some of the issues that Katia raises regarding concerns about her relationship with Marcus Sandford that also apply to Josie's relationship with Jacob, illustrating the enduring cultural conflict across generations.

Michael Andretti

Key quotes

'If you can't be honest, don't expect to stand up in a court room and defend honesty.' (p.88)

'I'm not sure if I can love you [Josie] ever, but I want to know you. I want to be part of your life.' (p.128)

'I ran away from commitment eighteen years ago. I should never have done what I did to your mother. I can't run away again.' (p.245)

Michael develops from a concept to a person over the course of the novel. He is initially just a name to Josie, rather than a living, breathing human, and his unexpected appearance adds another layer to the identity crisis Josie is experiencing.

Michael is presented as an ultimately good man, albeit a flawed one. Initially unwilling to allow Josie into his life, his attitude thaws and he becomes increasingly involved. By the end of the novel, it is notable that it is Michael, rather than Christina, who takes Josie for dinner after her speech night, illustrating the development in their relationship. Having come to fatherhood late and unexpectedly, he is clumsy in his interactions with Josie at times, but he is able to be honest and direct with her in a way that Christina cannot. Michael treats Josie like the young adult she is, because he has never known her as anything else, and this pushes her to be accountable, such as when he forces her to reveal what prompted her to hit Carly with the book.

Michael, like Christina, provides an adult perspective on the challenges of teenage life, as he is able to reflect on the mistakes he made and the person that he was, but with the wisdom afforded by age and experience.

John Barton

Key quotes

'I've always had to be the best because it's been expected of me.' (p.46)

'I don't know what I want out of my life, but I know what I don't want.' (p.47)

'I've got my whole future planned out the way I want it to be and there is nothing anyone can do to take that away from me.' (p.229)

On the surface, John is a character who has everything – good looks, intelligence, connections and wealth. As the son of a politician, and coming from a long line of politicians, his future success appears mapped out for him. This is certainly Josie's perception of him, but readers are positioned early on to see John's battles with the expectations that are placed on him. Like several of the characters within the novel, he acts as a warning against judging a book by its cover, as beneath the facade of success is a boy struggling to find his own path and a sense of individual identity. Unfortunately for John, he feels too trapped to be able to break free of the weight of expectations on him, and he takes the only option that he believes is available to him: taking his own life. Through John, Marchetta illustrates that challenges exist in every level of society, and that sometimes those who have everything on a material level may suffer from a lack of human connection.

Jacob Coote

Key quotes

'Well, what the hell are you? The other day you called me an Australian as if it was an insult. Now you're not an ethnic. You people should go back to your own country if you're so confused.' (p.123)

'You [Josie] think you're the first person to ever suffer. You think your life is so difficult. But it's *you* who makes it difficult.' (p.206)

'I don't want to do what other people think I'll end up doing. I don't want to be stereotyped because of the school I attend or the district I live in.' (p.251)

Portrayed initially as a bad boy who is everything John isn't, Jacob starts the novel as something of a stereotype and progresses into a well-rounded character who experiences growth and development alongside Josie.

As an attendee of Cook High, a public school, Jacob is positioned as inferior to most of the other teenagers in the novel. There is a snobbery in the way Josie treats him initially, yet he proves to be the character most capable of thought and self-reflection. His lower socioeconomic status may not have afforded him the privileges and opportunities available to some of the other characters, but he displays a resilience and determination that is commendable. Having lost his mother to cancer in his early teens, Jacob has faced real adversity and yet he develops into a caring, thoughtful and practical young man. On the surface he lacks sophistication, with his dishevelled appearance, fondness for bikes and quick temper but, as Josie discovers, his rough exterior hides a capacity for sensitivity and warmth. While we, as readers, are positioned to follow Josie's development, Jacob undergoes a similar change, becoming a young man who is questioning what more life can offer him, rather than simply accepting the hand that he has been dealt.

Jacob functions as a foil to Josie's prejudices, highlighting that she is as guilty of judging as she criticises others of being, and that she makes assumptions about 'Aussies' just as much as they do about 'ethnics'. Their different backgrounds highlight the divisions within Australian society, with Jacob's initial behaviour illustrating the prevalence of a lack of acceptance towards European migrants. Despite being depicted as a predominantly good person throughout the novel, he still uses derogatory remarks such as 'go back to your own country', highlighting that this was a common attitude within society. Jacob, to his credit, has a willingness to compromise and attempt to understand, and Marchetta presents him as a character from whom much can be learned.

Key point

Josie's relationship with Jacob runs parallel to the development of her relationship with Michael. There is a turbulence to their initial encounters, and neither relationship runs smoothly, but Josie is shown to learn from both of these new male presences in her life. Marchetta also highlights the potential for Josie and Jacob's relationship to follow a similar route to Christina and Michael's, especially with similarities such as the car Jacob buys being the same make as the one in which Josie was conceived.

Seraphina, Lee Taylor, Anna Selicic

Key quotes

'You must be so worried that what happened to your mother will happen to you. Wouldn't that be terrible? People would have a field day.' (Sera, p.137)

'People breed with their own kind ... The rich marry the rich, Josie, and the poor marry the poor.' (Lee, p.144)

'It is a loss of innocence you know ... I think it's the only thing you have left that belongs to you and that belongs to that cocoon of childhood.' (Lee, p.257)

While Josie's group of friends have separate and distinct personalities, they typically appear together and present varied views on key teenage topics addressed in the novel. Each of the friends share characteristics with Josie, but their differences are also significant, enabling them to provide a contrast to her perspective.

Sera is the most significant character of the three. She is extroverted, blunt and downright mean at times. The Italian heritage she shares with Josie is a double-edged sword, as it means she is able to understand the challenges Josie faces as an illegitimate child with no father, but it also means that she makes Josie uncomfortable at times with her comments about her background. Sera depicts some of the prejudice felt by the Italian community towards Josie. Sera is also the most sexually experienced of the friends and has a different attitude to sex to Josie. To her, like Jacob, sex is no big deal.

Anna is the counterpoint to Sera. Sheltered, naive and timid, she is the most emotionally sensitive and is protected by the other girls. The most reserved of the four, Anna is even less sexually outgoing than Josie. The lack of information revealed about her personality reflects her shy nature. She falls for Jacob's friend, Anton Valavic, and their relationship progresses slowly throughout the year.

Lee is presented as a kind of Anglo version of Josie, but with greater self-assurance. Other than her being a scholarship student like Josie, having an alcoholic father and sleeping with Matt at the end of the novel, we learn little about Lee. She acts as the middle ground in the friendship group, lacking both Sera's showiness and Anna's uncertainty, and having an outlook more similar to Josie's. As shown at the end of the novel when they discuss sex, Lee understands Josie and her tendency to overthink things, and they are able to talk openly with each other. While Lee doesn't have much to do in the novel, the conversations she has with Josie tend to be revealing.

Ivy Lloyd and Carly Bishop

Key quotes

'No matter how much I hate Poison Ivy, I want to belong to her world ... A world where I can be accepted.' (p.32)

'And you're more than a wog, if you know what I mean.' (Carly, p.82)

'Ivy doesn't have "one-offs". She's responsible from the moment she walks into this school till the moment she walks out.' (Sister Louise, p.182)

While Ivy and Carly are very different in personality, they play similar roles in representing aspects of society to which Josie aspires. With St. Martha's presented as a microcosm of Sydney (and, indeed, urban Australia more generally), Marchetta uses schoolyard rivalries to illustrate the stark divisions within society.

Carly Bishop plays a smaller role in the novel, as one of 'the beautiful people' (p.80) who believes that looks grant her value in society. Carly is presented as racist and judgemental and her appearance points to a narrow Anglocentric definition of beauty in the Australian society of the time.

Ivy Lloyd is presented as Josie's nemesis, the Anglo, moneyed, connected version of her who has everything that Josie desires. Competition between Josie and Ivy drives both of them, and their similarities are apparent to John, but not to either girl until after his death. Both are motivated by the desire to beat the other, but Josie is unable to see this in Ivy, as her view of Ivy is obscured by her belief that her status has already granted her success in life. While Ivy is aware of the responsibility that comes with leadership, her privileged background also gives her the confidence to succeed, meaning that she is not plagued with the same doubts about her capability as Josie.

Key point

The change in Josie's relationship with Ivy at the end of the novel helps to illustrate an aspect of Josie's emancipation. Note that Josie is accepting of Ivy being named dux at speech night, whereas previously she had been driven by 'how wonderful it is to beat Poison Ivy' (p.21). The end of the novel marks a kind of inversion of their relationship, with Ivy admitting that she 'worked harder because of [Josie]' (p.241).

Sister Louise

Key quotes

'You have to stop believing that your actions are always right and you have to remember that you aren't a leader because you're given a title. You're a leader because of what is inside of you.' (p.184)

'You have great potential, Josephine, but so do many others. It's up to you to use that potential.' (p.184)

Fittingly, given that she is a nun, Sister Louise acts as a moral yardstick against which Josie's actions are measured. While Josie largely views her as an adversary, Sister Louise holds Josie to account for her misbehaviour and transgressions, thereby challenging her to reach her potential and accept that leadership involves responsibility and sacrifice. Whether Josie likes it or not, Sister Louise acts as a mentor to her, and her revelation that she appointed Ivy as captain despite Josie getting more votes marks the beginning of Josie's emancipation.

Marcus Sandford

While not appearing physically in the action of the novel, Marcus Sandford plays a key role in driving the narrative. He is initially presented somewhat stereotypically, with a focus on his practicality and masculinity, because of his role in helping Katia and Patrizia while their husbands were interred. However, once his close relationship with Katia is revealed, she describes him in more tender, gentle terms, emphasising his sensitivity and their emotional connection. In this way, he provides a counterpoint to the cold, distant Francesco, who is presented as a selfish and uncaring husband.

THEMES, IDEAS & VALUES

Family and relationships

Key quotes

'I vowed ... I'll leave and never have anything to do with my family again.' (p.40)

'I will sit between them and be a link and I'll fight with all my might to see that nothing tears my family unit apart.' (pp.260–1)

Family is central to the novel, with much of the action focused on Josie's relationships with her mother, her grandmother and – gradually – her father. Marchetta explores the importance of such relationships in a person's life, and how they can be both beneficial and restricting, particularly to a teenager. The exploration of this theme is not, however, limited to the Alibrandi women, as different versions of family are presented through other characters, encouraging reflection on what is meant by family.

The relationships between the Alibrandi family members are depicted as close – at times, perhaps suffocatingly so – and there is a strong bond between them all. From the outset, the strength of Josie's relationship with Christina is clear, as they talk openly about difficult subjects, such as the return of Michael Andretti. Having never had to share her mother with anyone before, Josie is fiercely protective of her. Katia has a similar approach to Christina, often telling her how to behave to avoid the risk of gossip and judgement by the Italian community. This leads to conflict, as the different generations have different values and desires, and each of the women dislikes being told what to do by others. Josie initially views her family as a burden and feels constricted by the expectations and rules to which she has to adhere, vowing 'to leave and never have anything to do with [her] family again' (p.40). However, she learns the value of familial relationships as she develops a greater understanding of her mother and grandmother as individuals, through stories about Katia's migration and her mother's forced separation from her family.

The novel also explores the ways in which family relationships change over time. While Josie has a certain level of maturity at the beginning of the novel, she tends to see her mother and grandmother in quite narrow terms, and largely in regard to their relationship to her. This is clear when she becomes angry at Christina for wanting to go on a date with a man and to spend time socially with people her own age, as well as in her initial dismissal of Katia's 'boring Sicily stories' (p.17). Gradually, however, Josie begins to understand that Christina and Katia are fully rounded human beings themselves, and that they were once teenagers just like her, with hopes and dreams for the future. The arrival of Michael, along with Katia's recollections of her early years in Australia, provides opportunities for both women to recount their experiences when they were on the cusp of adulthood, and for Josie to realise that the challenges of growing up do not change much over generations. It is notable that, in the final chapters of the novel, Josie repeatedly refers to her mother and grandmother as 'women', illustrating that she now sees them as entities in their own right, rather than as just 'Mama' and 'Nonna'.

Despite having not known him for as long, Josie experiences a similar relationship development with Michael. Initially she views him in narrow, stereotypical terms, rejecting him outright, and then calling on him to rescue her when she breaks Carly Bishop's nose. She accuses Michael of being 'full of bullshit clichés' (p.69), but Josie at this point is just as guilty of having a clichéd concept of what 'father' means. Viewing him as some kind of protector, she calls on him to rescue her from the threat of litigation, and then basks in his reflected glory as they walk down the school corridor together. At the beginning of their relationship, she doesn't treat Michael as a person, but as a physical rebuke to all the bullies and name-callers who she feels have looked down on her illegitimacy – the fact that he is a barrister, and thus respectable, further adding to his status. However, as their relationship develops, Josie begins to see Michael as a complete person, just as she does with her mother and grandmother. By the end of the novel, Josie's descriptions of Michael are far more focused on his personality and their relationship, rather than on his job or other superficial aspects.

While Josie bemoans her family situation at times, wishing that she had a father and wasn't illegitimate, the depiction of other characters' families challenges the idea that having a conventional nuclear family set-up guarantees happiness. For example, while bully Greg Sims comes from a typical nuclear family, the 'screaming and yelling' and 'loud crying' (p.101) at night points to a deeply unhappy environment, and potentially domestic violence. Similarly, John Barton's relationship with his father is presented as cold and distant, as he is unable to talk about his aspirations and desires, ultimately leading to his suicide.

Identity

Key quotes

'That's why I want to be rich and influential. I want to flaunt my status in front of those people and say "See, look who I can become".' (p.138)

'You're just so confused about who you are that you feel that everyone is labelling you.' (Jacob, p.250)

As indicated by the title, the search for identity is intrinsic to this novel. Josie spends the events of the book struggling with who she is and trying to find her place in the world, common challenges for most people as they transition into adulthood. She grapples with the conflict between the perceived expectations placed on her by the outside world and her own desires, and has to find a way to balance these. While this struggle is apparent to readers from the outset of the novel, Josie initially believes that she has a clear sense of who she is, as evidenced when she introduces herself to readers in the opening chapter. It is, however, noticeable that this introduction relates entirely to the superficial and the extrinsic – her age, her background, her illegitimacy, the social status of her family etc. There is nothing that introduces Josie as a person, such as her values or the things that make her tick. Josie initially views herself as a series of labels, because that is how she thinks others see her, and as a result she constantly berates herself for not being good enough.

As the novel progresses, however, and her world view is challenged by various events, Josie begins to realise that many of the perceptions she has of herself are actually untrue. By casting herself as an unpopular outsider at school, Josie has essentially created that as a reality for herself, and we, as readers, are drawn to believe it as well. But Sister Louise upends Josie's perceptions when she reveals that she was actually voted school captain, and that she and her friends are considered 'trendsetters' (p.183). The burden of inferiority that Josie has carried is revealed to be a lie, and thus she is able to look at herself through fresh eyes. This understanding that how one views oneself and how one is viewed by others can be very different things is a key element within the novel.

Key point

Josie's initial description of herself may be superficial and based on labels, but this does not mean that the elements she refers to are irrelevant to her identity. Like all of us, Josie is a product of her environment. Her identity is shaped by her Italian–Australian heritage, by being brought up in inner Sydney by a single mother, by being a scholarship student etc. The point that Marchetta is making, and that Josie comes to understand by the end of the novel, is that these are factors that contribute to one's identity, but they do not define it. When Josie redefines herself in the closing chapter, the focus is on her perception of herself, and her own thoughts and feelings, rather than those of others. She has made peace with some of the conflicting aspects of her identity, noting that 'it matters who I feel like I am' (p.261).

While the first-person narrative voice inevitably guides readers to focus on Josie's search for identity, she is not the only character depicted as grappling with their sense of self. Although he appears to be perfect in many ways, John Barton struggles with the identity that has been foisted upon him by others, and is unable to align it with his personal perception of self. Tragically, his search for self ends in suicide, as he feels unable to break away from the external pressures shaping him into something that he doesn't want to be.

Marchetta also suggests that battling with one's identity is not restricted to teenagers. Christina's argument with Josie and Katia prior to her date with Paul Presilio reveals that she is desperate to be seen as a woman, rather than simply a mother or daughter. Josie learns to see Christina as a person throughout the course of the novel, as it explores her past, as well as her dreams and aspirations. Through the character of Christina, Marchetta highlights that identity is not a finite matter; rather, it is a process that is constantly being refined and reviewed as one moves through the different stages of life.

Growing up

Key quotes

'We'd never be able to cope with the pressures our mothers and grandmothers went through.' (p.79)

'I wish I was a little girl again.' (Lee, p.257)

As a coming-of-age novel focusing on a seventeen-year-old girl, there is inevitably an exploration of growing up and its associated challenges. This is heightened through the use of a first-person narrative style, which provides insight into the thoughts and feelings of Josie as she navigates her way through her final year of school.

While Josie's immediate responses to events throughout the novel tend to be emotional and impulsive, she becomes increasingly reflective and thoughtful in the aftermath, demonstrating a greater awareness of the impact of her behaviour and a capacity to see things from the perspective of others. Compare, for example, her response to the failed first date with Jacob – when she 'really wanted him to ring and apologise' (p.130) and then doesn't speak to him for an extended period – to her response to their later argument about introducing Jacob to her grandmother, when she goes to see him the next day. Her behaviour is still self-centred and far from perfect, as she asks him to 'be thankful [she] swallowed [her] pride', but she can at least acknowledge that she was 'taking the wrong approach' (p.208), demonstrating progression in her ability to see things from someone else's perspective.

Importantly, Josie continues to oscillate between maturity and immaturity throughout the novel, thus providing a realistic reflection of life as a teenager. While she demonstrates an emotional capacity to handle life-changing events such as the appearance of her father, her relationship with John exemplifies her immaturity. Her attraction to him is initially described in highly superficial terms. She fails to appreciate the depth of his emotional turmoil, becoming annoyed with him for talking negatively about life and noting that she 'wasn't as attracted to him as [she] used to be' (p.132). Josie's obliviousness to John's depressive state has tragic consequences in the novel, but it is also realistic – teenagers frequently are self-absorbed and unaware of those around them, and conversations around mental health were far less prevalent in the early 1990s when the novel is set. Josie's juvenility is emphasised through the language used in her reaction to John's death, referring to Christina as 'Mummy' (p.235) rather than 'Mama'. This is the only time she uses this term, which is typically associated with small children, thus depicting Josie as a scared child reaching for her mother in a time of emotional turmoil.

Josie's 'emancipation', as she terms it, comes as she gradually realises that she is the one holding herself back. Her developing maturity enables her to see that she has the ability to define herself, rather than being restricted by being defined by others. Through her relationship with Jacob, Josie realises that it is up to her to determine who she is, and whose opinions she concerns herself with. Presented as a no-nonsense, straight-talking character, Jacob has the ability to challenge Josie's preconceptions and prejudices. He calls her out for 'whinging and wailing about the way people treat [her]' but failing to think about the way she treats them in return (p.191), and suggests that her friendship with John is related to her desire to belong to 'the elite of the community' (p.193). His summation of her when they break up – 'You're just so confused about who you are that you feel that everyone is labelling you' (p.250) – is perhaps the most accurate description in the entire novel.

Key point

In keeping with the general realism of the writing, Josie is not presented as a perfectly polished grown-up by the end of novel, and it is left to readers to make the final call on the extent of her emancipation. While Josie has undoubtedly matured, she is still figuring out elements of herself. She finishes the novel by declaring that her emancipation has occurred; however, given the novel's first-person narrative style, and the unreliable nature of a seventeen-year-old narrator, readers must determine the extent to which they believe Josie's final statement: 'finally I understood' (p.261).

Expectations

Key quotes

'I tried to picture John Barton terrorising girls in alley ways or Jacob Coote being able to converse with the Premier. It made me so much more aware of the social and cultural differences around me.' (p.43)

'I've always had to be the best because it's been expected of me.' (John, p.46)

'Things aren't as easy for me as they are for you. You can do whatever you please but I can't because there are some things that could offend people I love. You live with such freedom, Jacob. You live without religion and culture. All you have to do is abide by the law.' (Josie, p.206)

The restrictive nature of expectations, and the constraints placed on people by society, are woven throughout the text, and are demonstrated to have a significant impact on the lives of a number of the characters. The impact of culture, social status, gender and history are all explored, as Marchetta examines the different elements that shape people and govern what they feel they can or can't do.

Cultural expectations

A key component of Josie's resentment of her Italian heritage is the constricting nature of behavioural expectations. As depicted in the early interactions with Nonna Katia, the need to dress and behave with decorum causes clashes across the Alibrandi family, as Josie is accused of being 'without respect' (p.36), leading her to rail against being stifled 'with ridiculous rules and regulations they have brought with them from Europe' (p.40). However, while she bemoans the expectations that are placed upon her by her culture, she still finds it impossible to break free of them. Her relationship with Jacob encounters many hiccups initially, as her expectations of him, and how a potential boyfriend has to behave, are very far removed from his own expectations. Josie feels obliged to adhere to the cultural expectations of her family, noting that 'they're waiting for me to make an error so they can compare me and my mother' (p.152).

Gender expectations

Expectations regarding gender are prevalent throughout the novel and are explored through the different generations of the Alibrandi family, whose members are restricted in the way they are allowed to behave. Katia's recollections of her life as a teenage bride illustrate a restrictive life where decisions are made by men – for example, her father's oldest brother 'decided that [she] should marry' (p.75). Christina suffers from a lack of freedom as a single mother, with the expectation that she will sacrifice her sense of self and devote everything to being a mother. When she does show interest in socialising and dating, she is criticised by both her mother and daughter for her behaviour, illustrating that judgement is not limited to those who are older and more traditional. While it is not explored in detail, there are clear differences in terms of the expectations placed on Josie compared to those placed on her cousin Robert. Both, for example, are depicted play-fighting in the pool at a family barbecue, but Josie is the one who is told to 'grow up', while Robert is described as 'a good boy' (p.64).

Expectations relating to social status and class

Social status and class also play a role in expectations, both visibly and covertly. For many of the students at St. Martha's and St. Anthony's, academic success and university admittance are expectations, and thus those teenagers are on a defined path to continuing the financial success of their parents. By contrast, there are fewer expectations on the likes of Jacob Coote, who 'used to be proud of not getting good marks' (p.249) and who doesn't place the same value on education because there is no pressure on him to be anything other than a mechanic. Marchetta highlights the confining nature of social expectations through Josie and Lee's discussion in Chapter 15, where Lee paints a depressing picture of the potential for social mobility. While Josie optimistically declares that they're 'masters of [their] own destiny', Lee asserts that 'people breed with their own kind … the rich marry the rich, Josie, and the poor marry the poor' (p.144), suggesting that there are limits to the freedom that people have to 'better' themselves from a socioeconomic perspective.

Although this view of limited social mobility may appear bleak, Marchetta also explores the challenges and restrictions faced by those among society's elite. Despite appearing – to Josie at least – to be completely in control and have everything going for him, John Barton struggles with the weight of expectation placed on him by his father, and feels utterly unable to break free. His suicide acts as a warning about the dangers of expectation, and how detrimental the impact of external pressure can be, particularly during one's formative years.

While differing in almost every way from John, and having grown up without the weight of expectation on his shoulders, Jacob is also presented as struggling with his future towards the end of the novel. Marchetta depicts him as initially self-assured and with a clear sense of his future, but his exposure to different ways of thinking through his relationship with Josie results in Jacob questioning what he wants from life. When Josie goes to visit, Jacob's father describes him as being aware 'of what he can and can't do' (p.209), suggesting that Jacob knows his limits and his place in society. This contrasts, however, with the end of the novel, where he acknowledges 'that there's more to life' (p.251) and expresses the need to explore his options.

Cultural conflict

Key quotes

'Ethnic is a word that you people use to put us all in a category.' (p.166)

'A different Australia emerged in the 1950s. A multicultural one, and thirty years on we're still trying to fit in as ethnics and we're still trying to fit the ethnics in as Australians.' (p.202)

While still generally multicultural, Sydney of the late 1980s and early 1990s was quite segregated in terms of ethnicity and in terms of how people viewed each other. European migration had changed the population of Australian cities significantly since World War II, and these first- and second-generation migrants were often viewed as 'New Australians', which had the effect of denoting them as different. The novel highlights the contemporary challenges of trying to come to terms with conflicting cultural expectations, while also exploring the historical issues faced by first-generation migrants.

Marchetta explores external cultural conflict through how Josie is viewed by Australians and Italians, and how this leads to internal conflict, as Josie is unsure of how to categorise herself. Josie recounts: 'my mother was born here so as far as the Italians were concerned we weren't completely one of them. Yet because my grandparents were born in Italy we weren't completely Australian' (p.7), illustrating the cultural confusion that both Josie and Christina would have experienced growing up. The lack of acceptance of European migrants by the wider Australian society is also manifested in more directly racist confrontations, such as in the playground at primary school (p.234), or through Josie's fight with Carly as a result of her labelling all southern Europeans as 'wogs' (p.81). The extent to which cultural prejudice exists within Australian society is highlighted by the range of characters who express similar sentiments, with both Ivy and Jacob referring to Josie as 'ethnic'.

Despite her anger at such views, Josie also sees herself as being different. She uses the term 'Australian' as an insult towards Jacob on several occasions, and notes that 'we live in the same country, but we're different' (p.152). Her difficulty in reconciling her cultural identities is at the heart of the novel.

The longevity of cultural conflict within Australia is explored through Katia's recounting of her experiences as a newly arrived migrant. She notes the initial culture shock of landing in Sydney and seeing women working in bars and experiencing catcalling from men. She also recounts how the Italian migrants 'lived in [their] own little world' and that, as their community grew, they 'didn't need to make friends with the Australians' (p.78). As Josie observes, little has changed in the ensuring decades as 'the same ignorance that was around back then is still here now' (p.79). Josie acknowledges the challenges of creating a multicultural society and apportions blame for the difficulties to both the migrant and existing Australian communities, noting that 'so many have stayed in their own little world. Some because they don't want to leave it, others because the world around them won't let them in' (p.202). While Josie is depicted as finding personal peace in terms of her cultural identity at the end of the novel, Marchetta recognises that the process is more complex for Australian society as a whole, which she expresses through Josie's observation: 'I'm not sure whether everyone in this country will ever understand multiculturalism and that saddens me, because it's as much part of Australian life as football and meat-pies' (p.258).

DIFFERENT INTERPRETATIONS

Different interpretations arise from different responses to a text. Over time, a text will evoke a wide range of responses from its readers, who may come from various social or cultural groups and live in very different places and historical periods. Responses by critics and reviewers can be published in newspapers, journals and books, both online and in print. They can also be expressed in discussions among readers in the media, classrooms, book groups and so on.

While there is no single correct reading or interpretation of a text, it is important to understand that an interpretation is more than a personal opinion – it is the justification of a point of view on the text. To present an interpretation of a text based on your point of view, you must use a logical argument and support it with relevant evidence from the text.

The critics' viewpoints

Despite the challenges that Melina Marchetta faced in initially getting the book published, when it was finally released in 1992 the first print run sold out in two months. It was an instant success, winning a number of literary awards, and it has continued to enjoy popularity ever since.

The novel was praised for its realistic depiction of teenage angst and effectively capturing an authentic adolescent voice. Alice Pung notes that the novel 'is the real deal' and that 'Josephine Alibrandi was someone [she] knew', applauding the novel for being 'a book that, in the tradition of J.D. Salinger and Vera Brittain, speaks about the vicissitudes of moody teenagers' (Pung 2013). Neha Kale also observed that Josie is 'one of the few characters in Australian literature that genuinely feels like an old friend' (Kale 2016).

Having a protagonist from a minority background was uncommon at the time of the book's publication, and it was even more rare to find that the character's ethnicity was not their sole defining feature. Pung acknowledges that the novel was 'ground-breaking', coming at a time when 'the shelves of libraries and bookstores still had the category "Ethnic Literature"', and she credits its importance in paving the way for her own writing, and allowing it 'to be read as a bildungsroman and not a refugee story' (Pung 2013). The importance of Marchetta's exploration of the displacement felt by second- and third-generation migrants and the development of a hybrid culture is also noted by Lana Zannettino, who comments that 'instead of having to choose between two cultures', characters such as Josie 'are able to embrace their cultural heritage in a flexible third space' (Zannettino 2007).

Interpretation 1: *Looking for Alibrandi* depicts the universal and timeless challenges of growing up.

The enduring popularity of *Looking for Alibrandi* over the thirty years since its original publication highlights the universality of its main message and themes. While the world has undoubtedly changed significantly since the book's publication in 1992, the core message about the difficulties faced by teenagers trying to establish their individual identity and find their place in an adult world remains as pertinent now as it did then.

For a young person growing up and attempting to establish an individual sense of self, family can be a source of both comfort and conflict. Within *Looking for Alibrandi*, Marchetta explores these elements, presenting the strong sense of love and affection that exists within the Alibrandi family – particularly between Christina and Josie – and also the conflict that arises over differences of opinion. From the outset, Christina and Josie's relationship is depicted as being close; they 'love each other to bits and spend hours in deep and meaningful conversation' but they are also capable of 'screeching at each other about the most ridiculous thing' (p.5). While not explored in as much detail, the references to Katia and Christina's relationship when the latter was a teenager highlight that intergenerational relationships have their highs and lows no matter the time period. Another family-related challenge explored in the novel is the transition that children must make to seeing their parents as people, rather than in an idealised way. Typically, as children, we view our parents as infallible, and therefore part of growing up is realising that they are human, and thus capable of error as well as good. Marchetta illustrates the difficulties Josie faces in accepting Christina's desire to date and have a social life, with the protagonist declaring, 'I never want it to be anything but her and me and I'm angry that she's even thinking of letting anyone else in' (p.99). While the specifics of the relationships between the characters may be influenced by time and heritage, the depiction of changing family dynamics is something that could apply to any family in any time period.

The importance of friends and relationships during one's teenage years is also a timeless concept. While Sera, Anna and Lee do not feature as prominently as some other characters, Marchetta highlights their importance to Josie by introducing them early in the novel. They are instantly recognisable characters, providing Josie with a sounding board when she is unsure, and the group has a realistic variety of opinions and perspectives that serves to remind readers of their own teenage friendship groups. Even the outlandish character of Sera and the complex nature of Josie's relationship with her is relatable, as the idea of having a friend who is both likeable and unlikeable may resonate with many. The concept of friendship being confined to fixed groups is something that has been explored extensively in literature and film across the years, and Josie's labelling of others at St. Martha's as 'the beautiful people', 'European trendies' or 'intellectuals' may remind readers of similar scenes in films such as *Mean Girls*. Aside from friendship, the novel's exploration of first love and sexual activity is relevant regardless of the decade. The intensity of Josie's feelings towards Jacob, admitting to readers her love for him after one date with him, realistically capture the emotional turbulence of young love, as does the later debate between Josie and Jacob about the physical progression of their relationship. Teenage years are characterised by intense relationships, both platonic and romantic, and Marchetta explores these through her protagonist's actions and inner thoughts.

With the novel focusing on the final year of Josie's schooling, the spectre of the future inevitably looms large, as it does for most students as they prepare to leave secondary education. Despite beginning the novel with a fixed plan for her post-school pathway, Josie ends the novel uncertain of whether she wants to be a barrister; similarly, Jacob begins to question his goal of becoming a mechanic. Through these characters and experiences, Marchetta highlights the universal nature of uncertainty, illustrating that it is not limited to certain socioeconomic groups or those with particular aspirations.

Interpretation 2: *Looking for Alibrandi* presents a snapshot in time, focusing on teenage life in 1990s Sydney.

Depicting an urban environment stringently divided by class and ethnicity, and a pre-digital world in which communication relies on landlines, *Looking for Alibrandi* is intrinsically rooted in the time and place of its setting, providing readers with a glimpse into recent Australian history.

In the novel, Josie's Italian heritage is a significant factor in the crisis of identity that she experiences. She struggles to reconcile the connection she feels to her family's background with her connection to Australia, the country of her birth and where she resides, and there is a sense that she is expected to choose to identify with just one of the nationalities. Through Josie, Marchetta presents an Australia in which distinction between European ethnic groups was far more prevalent than today, with terms such as 'New Australian', 'wog' and 'ethnic' used in a derogatory manner to indicate difference and outsider status. Josie's recounted experience from primary school encapsulates this, when she is teased by 'the Australian girls' who question her nationality and then reject her when she says she's Australian. Even the use of the phrase 'the Australian girls' to denote a specific group within the primary school highlights the division that exists, and there is a clear implication that this division is emblematic of attitudes across wider Australian society at the time. While racism and prejudice undoubtedly still exist within Australia today, negative attitudes to Australians of Italian descent have generally been consigned to history.

Most notably, *Looking for Alibrandi* presents a coming-of-age story that is based in a different – potentially more innocent – age, as it explores teenage life before the invention of the internet. While many of the concerns and challenges Josie and her friends face will be familiar to modern readers, their adolescence is markedly different in many ways to that experienced now. Scenes such as Josie enthusing that 'the time before class starts in the morning is the most exciting. Because we haven't seen each other for *sixteen* hours, it's gossip galore' (p.80) now appear quaint, given the interconnected nature of modern society. Equally, Jacob's comment to Josie that he's 'in the book. Only Coote in Redfern' (p.108) may cause confusion for readers unfamiliar with the concept of printed phone directories, and this also highlights the lack of personal phones, with everyone relying on the family's single landline for communication. Given Josie's self-doubt and struggles with her identity, it could be interesting to consider how a twenty-first-century version of the novel would look, in a world where teenagers are bombarded with media representations of perfection and unreality.

While much of what the novel explores in terms of family dynamics and the challenges of growing up remains pertinent no matter the time period, *Looking for Alibrandi* is a depiction of teenage life specifically in the early 1990s. Shifts in moral and societal attitudes, changes in cultural diversity and the advance of technology since the novel was written have irrevocably changed the Australian urban landscape, and thus this is a story that is firmly anchored in the past.

QUESTIONS & ANSWERS

This section focuses on your own analytical writing on the text, and gives you strategies for producing high-quality responses in your coursework and exam essays.

Essay writing – an overview

An essay on a literary work is a formal and serious piece of writing that presents your point of view on the text, usually in response to a given topic. Your 'point of view' in an essay is your interpretation of the meaning of the text's language, structure, characters, situations and events, supported by detailed analysis of textual evidence.

Analyse – don't summarise

In your essays it is important to avoid simply summarising what happens in a text.

- A **summary** is a description or paraphrase (retelling in different words) of the characters and events. For example: 'Macbeth has a horrifying vision of a dagger dripping with blood before he goes to murder King Duncan.'
- An **analysis** is an explanation of the real meaning or significance that lies 'beneath' the text's words (and images, for a film). For example: 'Macbeth's vision of a bloody dagger shows how deeply uneasy he is about the violent act he is contemplating, and conveys his sense that supernatural forces are impelling him to act.'

A limited amount of summary is sometimes necessary to let your reader know which part of the text you wish to discuss. However, always keep this to a minimum and follow it immediately with your analysis of what this part of the text is really telling us.

Plan your essay

Carefully plan your essay so that you have a clear idea of what you are going to say. The plan ensures that your ideas flow logically, that your argument remains consistent and that you stay on the topic. An essay plan should be a list of **brief dot points** covering no more than half a page.

- Include your central argument or main contention – a concise statement of your overall response to the topic.
- Write three or four dot points for each paragraph, indicating the main idea and evidence/examples from the text. In your essay you will need to *expand* on these points and *analyse* the evidence.

Structure your essay

An essay is a complete, self-contained piece of writing. It has a clear beginning (the introduction), middle (several body paragraphs) and end (the last paragraph or conclusion). It must also have a central argument that runs throughout, linking each paragraph to form a coherent whole. See examples of introductions and conclusions in the 'Analysing a sample topic' and 'Sample answer' sections.

The introduction establishes your overall response to the topic. It includes your main contention and outlines the main evidence you will refer to in the course of the essay. Write your introduction *after* you have done a plan and *before* you write the rest of the essay.

The body paragraphs argue your case – they present evidence from the text and explain how this evidence supports your argument. Each body paragraph needs:

- a strong **topic sentence** (usually the first sentence) that states the main point being made in the paragraph
- **evidence** from the text, including some brief quotations
- **analysis** of the textual evidence, with **explanation** of its significance and how it supports your argument
- **links back to the topic** in one or more statements, usually towards the end of the paragraph.

Connect the body paragraphs so that your discussion flows smoothly. Use some linking words and phrases such as 'similarly' and 'on the other hand', though don't start every paragraph like this. Another strategy is to use a significant word from the last sentence of one paragraph in the first sentence of the next.

Use key terms from the topic – or synonyms for them – throughout, so the relevance of your discussion to the topic is always clear.

The conclusion ties everything together and finishes the essay. It includes strong statements that emphasise your central argument and provide a clear response to the topic.

Avoid simply restating the points made earlier in the essay – this will end on a very flat note and imply that you have run out of ideas and vocabulary. The conclusion should be a logical extension of what you have written, not just a repetition or summary of it. Writing an effective conclusion can be a challenge. Try using these tips:

- Start by linking back to the final sentence of the second-last paragraph, rather than leaping to your main contention straight away – this helps your writing to flow.
- Use synonyms and expressions with equivalent meanings to vary your vocabulary. This allows you to reinforce your line of argument without being repetitive.
- When planning your essay, think of one or two broad statements or observations about the text's wider meaning. These should be related to the topic and your overall argument. Keep them for the conclusion, since they will give you something 'new' to say but still follow logically from your discussion. The introduction will be focused on the topic, but the conclusion can present a wider view of the text.

Essay topics

1. How does *Looking for Alibrandi* depict the challenges faced by migrants in a supposedly multicultural society?
2. '*Looking for Alibrandi* suggests that family can be both a blessing and a curse.'
   Discuss.
3. At the end of the novel Josie believes she has been emancipated. To what extent do you believe this to be true?
4. How are the competing demands on Josie portrayed by Marchetta within the novel?
5. '*Looking for Alibrandi* is a novel about Australia.'
   Discuss.
6. '*Looking for Alibrandi* suggests that family plays the most important role in determining one's identity.'
   Do you agree?
7. How does Melina Marchetta portray the challenges of growing up?
8. '*Looking for Alibrandi* suggests that self-acceptance is a lifelong process.'
   Discuss.
9. 'All of the characters in *Looking for Alibrandi* question who they are.'
   Do you agree?
10. '*Looking for Alibrandi* warns against the dangers of judging others based on their appearance.'
    Discuss.

Analysing a sample topic

'*Looking for Alibrandi* warns against the dangers of judging others based on their appearance.' Discuss.

With any topic, a good way to start is by turning it into a simple question, in order to give yourself a starting point for your contention. Here, this would result in the topic becoming, '**Does** *Looking for Alibrandi* warn about the dangers of judging by appearances?' Next, consider your response to that question to help you develop a contention, and begin to establish some supporting arguments. Given that this is a 'discuss' topic, you have a degree of freedom in how to frame your response – you could agree with the topic entirely or agree partially and challenge elements of the statement. It would, however, be difficult to completely disagree, given the content of the novel.

Once you've got a rough idea of the direction of your essay, the next step is to interrogate the topic by breaking it into its constituent parts. For example, the word 'appearance' most commonly relates to how something looks, so this is likely to be an aspect covered in your response. It can also relate to how something *seems*, which is a connected idea, but not exactly the same. Considering the difference between looking and seeming provides scope for a broader range of arguments to explore. The word 'dangers' is also key here. You should consider what constitutes a danger, and who is threatened by it. The word 'warn' is similarly significant – the topic isn't just asking if the novel *depicts* these dangers, it's asking if it cautions readers about them, so you must make sure that you address this in your response.

The plan below outlines one possible response to this topic. Here, the contention accepts the topic, but the essay explores the different ways that the novel could be seen as providing a warning.

Sample introduction

> The idea that appearances can be deceiving, and thus potentially dangerous, is explored by Melina Marchetta in her coming-of-age novel, *Looking for Alibrandi*. As her protagonist attempts to navigate her way from adolescence to adulthood, Marchetta unpacks the negatives that can result from judging a person on their outward appearance, and how external appearance and internal identity can

differ significantly. She also suggests that appearance can be restrictive, limiting the potential for both individual and societal growth. Ultimately, while Marchetta acknowledges that it is human nature to interpret situations and people based on appearance, she cautions against it being the defining feature of interactions and relationships.

Body paragraph outline

Body paragraph 1: The novel suggests that judging others based on their outward appearance can have negative consequences.

- Through Josie's first-person narration, readers hear a lot about her perception of others, often based on their outward appearance – especially early in the novel.
- Josie's perception of John is that he is perfect, because physically, socially and materially he has it all; however, this prevents her from being able to see how troubled and lost he is.
- Josie also judges Jacob because of his external appearance, viewing him as disrespectful and uncouth due to his clothing and interests. This causes issues in their relationship – such as being unwilling to introduce Jacob to Nonna – because of her inability to look past this.

Body paragraph 2: Marchetta explores how external perspectives may differ from how individuals perceive themselves, leading to misunderstanding or conflict.

- Josie feels insecure and disconnected, but is actually admired by others. Marchetta's use of first-person perspective helps to highlight this by allowing readers access to the protagonist's thoughts and feelings.
- Katia seems rigid and obsessive about rules, but revelation of her relationship with Marcus Sandford illustrates that there's more to her than is apparent.

→

- John Barton appears to have it all, but he is deeply unhappy and confused, and feels he has no freedom to choose his own path.
- Marchetta illustrates the prevalence of these misconceptions by having a range of characters express their views on others – for example, John views Josie as not having 'any pressures in life' (p.46), and Josie believes that Jacob has no rules he has to follow except the law (p.206).

Body paragraph 3: The novel cautions against the restrictive nature of judging others by their appearance, and how it can limit the potential for growth.

- Throughout the novel there are multiple references to homogenised groups – 'clone groups', 'ethnics', 'beautiful people', 'wogs' – and the terms are shown to be limiting and reductive.
- Lee's assessment of what she perceives as societal restrictions (p.144) highlights the prevalence of such views – that people have a place based on how they appear to others.
- This is explored more personally through Jacob's view of his limited opportunities: 'I don't want to do what other people think I'll end up doing' (p.251).

Sample conclusion

Through her depiction of a year in the life of Josephine Alibrandi, Melina Marchetta explores ideas of appearance and identity, and encourages readers to consider the wider societal impact of these concepts. She suggests that judgement based solely on external factors – whether physical, social or material – can be highly dangerous, and she urges consideration of how internal identity and external perception can be markedly different. Ultimately, she highlights the restrictive nature of appearance, both individually and on a societal level, encouraging readers to consider the dangers of pigeonholing either oneself or others based on preconceptions of background, class or physical features.

SAMPLE ANSWER

'*Looking for Alibrandi* suggests that family can be both a blessing and a curse.'
Discuss.

Family is central to Melina Marchetta's coming-of-age novel, *Looking for Alibrandi*. Following Josie Alibrandi, the novel's protagonist, and her search for identity, the text explores the way in which heritage and family history can be both beneficial and restrictive. Through her depiction of the trials and tribulations of the Alibrandi family and other characters, Marchetta highlights the complexities of familial relations and suggests that these relationships will have both positive and negative elements.

Marchetta outlines how relationships within families can be both causes of and solutions to emotional turmoil. Throughout the novel, the Alibrandi family is depicted as turbulent, with relationships seesawing from one emotional extreme to the other. Christina and Katia have a fraught relationship, resulting from Francesco's coldness towards Christina, and Katia's support of him out of a sense of guilt due to her infidelity. The secret of Christina's true parentage creates a gulf between them, which Christina cannot understand. In one of many examples of their clashes, Katia is critical of Christina's intention of going on a date, arguing that 'people will talk' about her 'gallivanting around the place' and that her actions will affect both Katia and Josie, while Christina is 'tired of being old' and wants to 'do something without [Katia] making [her] feel as if it was wrong'. While Josie and Christina have a similarly intense relationship, with Josie going as far as to tell her mother, 'I hope I die during the night and you regret it for the rest of your life', the lack of secrets between them results in a far warmer and healthier relationship. Even though they argue and exchange strong words, they are able to reconcile relatively quickly and discuss their feelings. The importance of the relationship is clear after the death of John Barton, as we see Josie turn to her mother for comfort and support, rather than her friends. Through the depiction of the two central mother-daughter relationships, Marchetta highlights the benefits and challenges that such family connections can bring, and also champions the importance of honesty in relationships, emphasising the emotional damage that can result from keeping secrets.

The novel suggests that family can provide a connection to heritage and history, which can be both grounding and suffocating. Josie's cultural identity as an Australian of Italian background results in her struggling to establish a sense of belonging, as she finds it difficult to reconcile the apparently conflicting expectations of her family and society. Initially, her family heritage is presented as a burden, with a focus on the 'ridiculous rules and regulations they have brought with them from Europe', but as the novel progresses, Josie comes to terms with her background. By the time 'Tomato Day' is depicted, Josie is more accepting of the importance of family history, acknowledging that 'culture is nailed into you so deep you can't escape it'. Marchetta also presents the positives of shared family history through Katia's recollections. Isolated in Queensland and away from all that she has grown up with, Katia experiences extreme loneliness, but the arrival of her sister provides her with connection to her past, and the closeness of their relationship is evident in their behaviour at family events several decades later as they finish each other's sentences and recount the same stories. By contrast, John Barton's family history is depicted as a curse, despite it offering material comfort. The expectation to 'follow in [his] father's footsteps', having come from a long line of politicians, proves to be suffocating. The pressures that John feels as a result of his family history proves to be inescapable, leading ultimately to his suicide. Through depicting both the beneficial and detrimental effects of family heritage, Marchetta emphasises the challenges of managing the conflicting external and internal demands when one is attempting to establish an individual identity.

Furthermore, Marchetta illustrates how family can have both positive and negative impacts on one's future from a societal perspective. She suggests that the family into which one is born has a wide-ranging influence on a person's future. In this regard, family may be a blessing or a curse, depending on the circumstances of the family. While the major focus in terms of family is on the Alibrandis, Marchetta also explores the varied impact of family through other characters. Lee's perspective on the long-term legacy of family, for example, paints a somewhat depressing picture regarding the challenges of social mobility. She argues that 'people breed with their own kind' meaning that 'we all end up where we started', and she firmly believes she'll 'probably be exactly the same' as her parents. While Josie challenges this view of the world, arguing that they are 'masters of [their] own destiny', the novel supports Lee's view to a certain extent, with few characters able to break free of their family legacy: Lee herself is introduced as someone who 'thinks it's cool to come to school with a hangover', despite having an alcoholic father; Greg Sims is presented as a violent bully in the same way as his father; Jacob is pursuing a career as a mechanic, similar to his brother-in-law; and it is even suggested that Josie is 'going to be a barrister because of [her] father', despite his absence from her life. Josie also acknowledges that she can never be with John Barton, as their 'families had nothing in common'. Through her depiction of a range of characters from different socioeconomic backgrounds being apparently restricted by their family situation, Marchetta highlights both the long-lasting influence of family and the challenges of social mobility within modern Australian society.

Throughout the novel, Marchetta presents the positives and negatives of familial relationships, how they can be a connection to heritage for better or worse, and the role that they can play in determining one's future. Her exploration of a range of relationships and the wider concept of 'family' itself emphasises the formative role it plays in shaping identity, and how this influence – good or bad – can last well into adulthood.

REFERENCES & READING

Text

Marchetta, M 1992, *Looking for Alibrandi*, Penguin Books Australia, Sydney.

Film

Looking for Alibrandi 2000, dir. Kate Woods, Robin Kershaw Productions. Starring Pia Miranda.

References and further reading

Kale, N 2016, '*Looking for Alibrandi* author on minorities, identity and her latest book', *SBS*, 22 November, https://www.sbs.com.au/topics/voices/culture/article/2016/11/21/looking-alibrandi-author-minorities-identity-and-her-latest-book

Marchetta, M 2022, 'Thirty years on, I'm still grappling with what *Looking for Alibrandi* means to me', *The Sydney Morning Herald*, 28 September, https://www.smh.com.au/culture/books/thirty-years-on-i-m-still-grappling-with-what-looking-for-alibrandi-means-to-me-20220919-p5bj6o.html

Pung, A 2013, '*Looking for Alibrandi*: Essay by Alice Pung', Readings, https://readingaustralia.com.au/essays/looking-for-alibrandi/

Zannettino, Z 2007, 'From "Looking for Alibrandi" to "Does my Head Look Big in This?": The role of Australian teenage novels in reconceptualising racialised-gendered identities', in *Transforming Cultures eJournal*, vol. 2, no. 1, https://epress.lib.uts.edu.au/journals/index.php/TfC/issue/view/39